PRAISE FOR FRE

Provocative and prophetic, Michael Waters pro____
issues that impact our communities, families, and the future of our country.
Through his political critique, you hear the voice of a street prophet. Through his
analysis of hip-hop, you hear the voice of a cultural connoisseur. Through
his reflections as a father, you hear the voice of a loving parent. FREESTYLE is
inspiring, convicting, educating—and in the end, uplifting.

—**Romal Tune**, author of *God's Graffiti: Inspiring Stories for Teens*

FREESTYLE is a thoughtful snapshot into the life of one of our preachers looking
at our 21st-century world through the lens of Christian hope. His musings
are poignant, prophetic, and thought-provoking and will remind you of days
gone by, the present, and what lingers on the horizon of tomorrow.

—**Bishop Vashti Murphy McKenzie**
Presiding Prelate, 10th Episcopal District
African Methodist Episcopal Church

Michael W. Waters is a gifted pastor, theologian, and community activist who is
uniquely qualified to provide a relevant, insightful, and challenging commentary
on some of the contemporary social and spiritual issues that confront the
church and community. In this book we do not hear from a detached spectator
but from one who is passionately involved in the confrontation, pointing the way
forward with a word of hope and reconciliation.

—**Zan W. Holmes Jr.**, pastor emeritus
St. Luke Community United Methodist Church, Dallas, Texas

FREESTYLE is a must read. Dr. Waters's ability to synthesize intellectual insight,
pastoral experience, and cultural insight is a rare gift. Song lyrics and scripture both
find themselves interwoven in a tapestry of hope, faith, and joy. He has shaped a
message that will bless both the suites and the streets.

—**Rev. Tony Lee**, founder and senior pastor
Community of Hope A.M.E. Church
Hillcrest Heights, Maryland

Michael Waters has drawn on his considerable pastoral leadership to compose a clear, evocative, challenging, and persuasive statement on how to be a Christian global citizen in a fractious world. FREESTYLE provides the reader with impressive and intelligent reflection on national issues, faith, family, popular culture, social ethics, and spiritual growth.

—**Harold J. Recinos**, PhD

Professor of Church and Society

Perkins School of Theology, Southern Methodist University

Rev. Waters draws you into pondering issues of justice, love, family, and faith with captivating prose and wisdom. I love the movement of each section: Check One— blog—Check Two and Cypher. He is authentically "born" of hip-hop and wise beyond his years. This book communicates to all regardless of age, race, gender, or circumstance if they are willing to engage in FREESTYLE.

—**Evelyn L. Parker**, PhD

Associate Dean for Academic Affairs

Perkins School of Theology

FREESTYLE

REFLECTIONS ON FAITH, FAMILY, JUSTICE, AND POP CULTURE

MICHAEL W. WATERS

FRESH AIR BOOKS®

Nashville

The Fresh Air® website http://www.freshairbooks.org

Fresh Air Books® is an imprint of Upper Room Books®. Fresh Air Books® and design
logos are trademarks owned by The Upper Room®, a ministry of GBOD®, Nashville,
Tennessee. All rights reserved.

Scripture quotations are from the New Revised Standard Version Bible, copyright 1989,
Division of Christian Education of the National Council of the Churches of Christ in the
United States of America, unless otherwise noted. Used by permission. All rights reserved.

Scripture quotations marked (TODAY'S NIV) are taken from the Holy Bible, New
International Version®, NIV®. Copyright © 1973, 1978, 1984, 2011 by Biblica, Inc.™ Used
by permission of Zondervan. All rights reserved worldwide. www.zondervan.com

At the time of publication all websites referenced in this book were valid. However, due
to the fluid nature of the Internet, some addresses may have changed or the content may no
longer be relevant.

"They Reminisce Over You (T.R.O.Y.), My God!" and "Coming of Age in the Age of
9/11" originally published in *Dallas South News*

Cover and interior design: Marc Whitaker/www.mtwdesign.net
Photo on cover and on About the Author page: Chris McBrown/nepstudio.com

LIBRARY OF CONGRESS CATALOGING-IN-PUBLICATION DATA

Waters, Michael W.
    Freestyle : reflections on faith, family, justice, and pop culture / Michael W. Waters.
        pages cm
    ISBN 978-1-935205-19-7 (print) — ISBN 978-1-935205-20-3 (mobi) —
    ISBN 978-1-935205-21-0 (epub)
    1. Theology, Doctrinal—Popular works. 2. Faith. 3. Family—Religious aspects—Christi-
anity. 4. Justice—Religious aspects—Christianity. 5. Popular culture—Religious aspects—
Christianity. I. Title.
    BT77.W36 2014
    261--dc23
                                                                                    2013024363

Printed in the United States of America

FOR

YULISE

My partner in life and ministry,
with whom many of the ideas contained herein were first shared,
by whom these drafts were first edited, and because of
whom life has been made much sweeter.

I love you!

ACKNOWLEDGMENTS

I must acknowledge several persons whose support has made this volume possible. To Shawn P. Williams, former editor of *Dallas South News*, for introducing me to blogging through his invitation to write for the religion section of his blog, thus allowing me to exercise and build my writing skills. To my college classmate Lakisha Carr, writer for the *New York Times*, who provided early critiques of my blogs. To Rev. Romal J. Tune, who introduced my blogging to the Huffington Post. To Rev. Matthew Wesley Williams, for offering critique to "An Odd Future for Faith in Hip-Hop," my first HuffPost blog prompting national attention. To Lucette Jefferson, former editor at the Huffington Post, for showing great interest in my blogs and providing tremendous support of these writings. And to the members of Joy Tabernacle African Methodist Episcopal Church: You have encouraged and supported your pastor each step of the way.

I am also indebted to the tremendous staff at Upper Room Books who believed these musings deserve publication. To Jill Ridenour, whose initiative at Upper Room proved the genesis to the manuscript's acceptance. And to a new and dear Birminghamian friend whose close edits and encouragement guided me along the final leg of the journey. Thank you!

Finally, to my children: Michael Jeremiah, Hope Yulise, and Liberty Grace. Your mere presence gives testimony to the majesty of God. Your lives have given mine greater meaning and purpose. And my hope that you will inherit a kinder, more peace-filled and loving world fuels my calling. Daddy loves you!

God bless you all!

CONTENTS

FOREWORD

I have known our author, the Rev. Dr. Michael W. Waters, most of his life. Even as a boy, he was extraordinarily gifted. He very openly expressed his love for his family, for God, and for learning. This young person loved people, and people loved him in return. After observing this young life that was so wonderfully endowed with outstanding gifts and graces, I began referring to him as a Son of Destiny. I have had the privilege of a front-row seat, watching him grow as a scholar, a husband and father, a Christian theologian, a churchman, and a relevant voice for his generation. With FREESTYLE, Dr. Waters fulfills my early prophecy: He is a Son of Destiny.

This age has been referred to as the Information Age, because information streams into our lives constantly. Today's events are passed on to us instantly, whether they are taking place in the next block or thousands of miles away. However, so much that is passed on to us seems to be slanted toward the negative. We hear of wars and gang violence, incidents that suggest racism and sexism, schools that do a poor job of teaching, and police departments that do a poor job of protecting. Scandals abound from the Church House to the State House. News of broken criminal justice, health care, and political systems bombards us. Media informs us that illicit drug use and alcoholism, suicide, homicide, divorce, pornography, rape, corporate corruption, and bullying are all on the increase.

In the midst of this avalanche of negative information, Michael W. Waters shares with his readers a powerful, relevant, and creative word of hope. Even as our author speaks optimistically to today's issues, it is clear that this prophet does not have his head in the sand, nor is he observing the world through rose-colored glasses. He sees the challenges, observes the pain, and is keenly aware of human failures; yet, he has hope. In this volume you will learn how he uses today's media to share some good news. Michael Waters is a new-day prophet who uses the social media of his generation. He is a blogger who has managed to use this vehicle to teach, correct, and inspire. His blog posts have reached a multitude of people from diverse backgrounds.

Dr. Waters's writing style is winning him strong support across this nation and globally, but more enchanting than his style is his content. He has carved out four broad areas to reflect on: faith, family, justice, and pop culture. In these areas he takes us on a guided tour and helps us discover the pockets of hope. Our author's hope is clearly rooted in his Christian faith. He unearths some tried truths, but his approach is fresh and new and gives us a different perspective.

I predict that Michael Waters's FREESTYLE will make its way to university classrooms, church Bible studies, youth retreats, and individuals both young and old who are open to powerful insights on hope. The Rev. Jesse Louis Jackson, traveling this nation for years, has encouraged his audiences to "keep hope alive." Be reassured, Jesse, the Rev. Dr. Michael W. Waters has heard you loud and clear.

—The Right Reverend John R. Bryant
Senior Bishop, African Methodist Episcopal Church

CHECK ONE, CHECK TWO
AN INVITATION TO THE CYPHER

Like an ever-increasing number of people, I get my news primarily by way of the Internet. I want new information, love to dialogue about it with others as well as understand how to apply to life what I learn. A few years ago, I found myself engaged in reading the Huffington Post (HuffPost), one of America's most popular news blogs. Never would I have imagined at that time that I would soon become a contributing writer to HuffPost.

It happened June 2011, in New Orleans, Louisiana, at the Fund for Theological Education's Leaders in Ministry Conference, where I was attending a day of media training. Our facilitator informed our group that he had connections at HuffPost—and that he would be willing to share those connections. The seed was sown for my first HuffPost blog. I returned to Dallas, inspired to pursue this tremendous opportunity. But first, I needed to write something worthy of publication.

As providence would have it, one of our church's new ministry partners invited me to write an education blog. And the organization thought so highly of the piece that they submitted it to HuffPost. Not only did HuffPost publish that blog, but they also extended me an invitation to become a contributing HuffPost blogger!

There was no particular science to my blogs. I simply began writing about issues and concerns of interest to me. I wrote about my family, popular culture, ministry, national issues—anything that intrigued or inspired me. Amazingly, others began to take interest in those writings too.

What resulted from all this is still, at times, hard for me to comprehend. National and international television, radio, and print media began sending e-mails and calling for interviews. Radio hosts began to read my blogs on air. Numerous online news sources picked up and posted my blogs. Teachers used my blogs in their classrooms. University professors engaged my blogs as part of their syllabi. Individuals from around the world contacted me to tell me how my words had made an impact on them. Most humbling, parents used my blogs to provide life lessons for their children and notified me of the same.

The presence of hope connects the reader to my writing more than anything else. I do not overlook the reality of evil's presence in our world, or its painful effects. I do not shy away from speaking uncomfortable truths. My writings often present a challenge: to be transformed for the good and to transform society for the good. Even in the face of evil, pain, and uncomfortable truths, I write of the hope present in the coming of a new and brighter day for all people.

Although I am a preacher and pastor, I seek not to be preachy in my presentation but to engage these subject matters as a concerned world citizen, convinced—as the Indian proponent of nonviolent change Mahatma Gandhi once spoke—that we must become the change we desire to see in the world.[1] Perhaps I have thus far received no greater response to my writing than from a man who noted that he had been following my work. About one particular offering, he comments in this way:

> I am not a religious person, more agnostic; yet I just love the writing of Pastor Michael W. Waters. We see so much hate from religious groups . . . and the like that it can sometimes overshadow all the Christians that live lives of love and kindness. Giving a voice to Christians like Michael W. Waters is so important. Who know[s] the future of my religious path? But because of people like this writer I can have respect and admiration for Christians and am at least open to studying the Bible. As always, beautifully written, Sir.[2]

Being a contributor to HuffPost has literally enabled me to share hopeful ideals with the world. And I am now elated to share several of these writings from this group, with expanded writings—with the hope that this will create new opportunities to engage, dialogue, and inspire each reader to manifest hope in our world.

A HOPE AND A FUTURE

I view life through the lens of Christian hope. I believe humankind's purpose is to inspire and to manifest hope each day: hope in a newer and brighter day in the face of darkness, hope in the ultimate victory of good over evil, and hope in the fulfillment of each one of God's promises toward us. A significant aspect of my writing intends to inspire

Christian hope in readers and to encourage active participation in promoting Christian hope within their respective communities and beyond.

I discern a particular call to inspire Christian hope in those who live in the urban center and to those who help, provide relief, and minister within this context where it often appears that hope is bankrupt. Many of these communities are overrun by violence, crime, poverty, and disease. As such, these communities can appear hopeless. FREESTYLE seeks to restore Christian hope by pointing toward the active presence of God at work within these communities, to renew the hope of a better day.

MY VOICE

I humbly offer a voice largely absent from the public square. I am a member of the first hip-hop generation, and my voice has been shaped by myriad experiences as an African American man in his early thirties, seminary trained and doctoral degree holding. Therefore, I am as comfortable in exegeting the works of Tupac Shakur as I am the epistles of the apostle Paul.

I am a fifth-generation ordained minister and founding pastor of one of my denomination's fastest-growing congregations in Texas, Joy Tabernacle African Methodist Episcopal Church. Joy Tabernacle is also the first successful AME church plant in Dallas, Texas, in nearly half a century and the first established in the new millennium in this, the nation's ninth largest city. In addition to the pastorate, I have worked in corporate America, party politics, and higher education.

I am married to my college sweetheart, Yulise, who is a practicing attorney. We are the parents of three young children at the time of this writing. We have lived, raised our family, and pastored in the urban center for the last seven years. When I write, I do so as one shaped by a deep and abiding faith, a love for family, rigorous academic study, a post-civil rights era racial politic, a hip-hop aesthetic, and a firsthand awareness of the joys and perils of life in the urban center. Each of these realities has shaped me and my writing voice.

MY FLOW

You'll find blogs in four hope-filled sections: faith, family, justice, and pop culture. In each section "Check One" and "Check Two" act as bookends for each original HuffPost blog. In the world of hip-hop, many freestyle artists have been known to speak, "Check one, check two!" into the microphone. The phrasing serves two purposes: (1) to put the freestyle artist on rhythm with the beat and (2) to encourage his or her audience to give undivided attention as the freestyle artist begins to flow, or rap, spontaneous lyrics.

For the purposes of FREESTYLE, "Check One" seeks to set the context of and the inspiration for the original blog. "Check Two" seeks to offer my learning and experience since writing the blog and to point to where I see God's active presence manifesting hope in the world.

Also, each offering concludes with a "Cypher." In hip-hop, a *cypher* is a gathering of freestylers whose voices flow and who listen to the flow from others. Creative force empowers this intimate dialogue. In FREESTYLE, the intimate dialogue is prayer, God's creative force calling us to help manifest hope in the world.

Finally, FREESTYLE invites you to "keep the flow" by responding to God's creative call.

Welcome to FREESTYLE! Join me as we meet with God, keep the flow, and together manifest hope in our world!

—Reverend Dr. Michael W. Waters

PART ONE

FAITH

FAITH

My father is an ordained minister who pastored several churches in Texas and California, spanning a thirty-year pastoral career and later serving as a New Testament scholar. In fact, he is one of relatively few African Americans who hold a PhD in New Testament studies. On my mother's side of the family, I am a fifth-generation ordained minister. Both of my maternal grandparents were pastors' children. Over many generations, seemingly countless uncles, aunts, and cousins have been ministers in the church.

Those family members outside ordained ministry also have been serving well. From church musicians to groundskeepers, missionaries to Sunday school teachers, my family has a great heritage of faith. The church my maternal grandfather attended as a child started in his grandmother's home almost a century ago. The congregation is still going strong.

Faith and praxis have long been central to my life and identity. As a young child, I was known to line up my stuffed animals at home and pretend to offer them Communion. I also tried my hand at directing choir from the pews. My former Sunday school teacher, now a pastor, has publicly stated that having me as a student in primary class forced her to study our lessons all the more closely. I was an inquisitive child who asked challenging biblical and theological questions.

When I was eleven years old, I sensed a call to ministry. At first, I did not understand what this call would entail, but I knew God had called me to preach. I also knew my purpose and destiny would be to serve others.

I've been preaching sixteen years now, pastoring for ten, have three degrees in religion; my theological inquiry has yet to subside. If anything, my exploration has intensified! In every circumstance, I seek to identify not only where God is actively present, but also where signs of hope are emerging.

Such a Christ-centered worldview might place me at odds with some, but I have always taken seriously the claim that God in Christ "is before all things, and in him all things hold together" (Col. 1:17).

My faith is my foundation.

THEY REMINISCE OVER YOU (T.R.O.Y), MY GOD!

CHECK ONE

The US civil rights movement has fascinated me since my youth. I would devour every fact that I could get my hands on. As early as the fifth grade, I completed a history project on the lynching of Black people in the early twentieth century. This created some challenges for me as I often had to fend off disturbing images during sleep. It also proved exceedingly difficult for my young mind to comprehend why some people held such hatred for others because of skin color. I found it impossible, however, to disengage from this material as the force and concern that drew me in were greater than any force or concern that would repel.

As I matured, my fascination for the movement did not change, although my emotional investment in the movement did. The images will never become easier to digest. But instead of seeing only the pain and horror as I did as a child, I grew to see the strength of a people guided by faith, who not only endured such great tragedy but who also emerged from it victorious.

As I matured, the images of the struggle became a point of sacred witness, and the necessity of passing down the story of the movement became paramount in my purpose. Over the years, I have been blessed not only to visit many of the historic sites of the movement but also to meet, to sit together, and to break bread with many leaders and foot soldiers of the movement. And I have sought to share all that they have shared with me, hoping that a new generation will know of the faith of their forebears, and find the faith to overcome the challenges of *our* day.

"Déjà vu, tell you what I'm gonna do, when they reminisce over you, my God."

—from "They Reminisce Over You (T.R.O.Y.)," Pete Rock and CL Smooth, 1992

On September 15, 1963, 10:22 AM, a bomb ripped through the Sixteenth Street Baptist Church of Birmingham, Alabama, moments before Sunday morning worship was to commence. In the blast's wake, four young girls, Addie Mae Collins (age 14), Cynthia Wesley (age 14), Carole Robertson (age 14), and Denise McNair (age 11), lay dead. Twenty-two other individuals sustained injuries from this domestic terrorist attack. One of the most heinous crimes committed in an era rife with them, the death of innocents and the utter disregard for the sacredness of a house of worship by so-called Christian segregation extremists resulted in an international outcry.

Though the story is well documented, often lost in the historicity of this tragedy is its enduring humanity: those left behind to grieve and mourn life lost and security disturbed. That day, parents lost their children, siblings their sisters, and a faith community, for years to come, its ability to worship with peace of heart and mind at its church building. Enter the Collins family. On that fateful day in September 1963, possibly no family and its members suffered more than they did. A family living in poverty, not only did they lose Addie Mae, but another child, Sarah, lost an eye. A third child escaped the blast with her physical life intact, but her life would remain on emotional life support for decades.

Junie Collins Williams, then sixteen, narrowly escaped death and injury through sheer obedience. When instructed by an elder to leave the church's downstairs lobby and return upstairs, she did not hesitate. She had piano-playing duties on that Sunday, which was Youth Sunday. Moments later, the bomb exploded. Four bodies, including that of her sister, were later discovered lying on top of one another under the rubble where the women's restroom had once stood. Ms. Williams was later given the horrific task of identifying her baby sister's body, which proved difficult to fulfill. The blast had so damaged Addie Mae's body and disfigured her face that it had rendered her unrecognizable. Ms. Williams was able to make a positive identification based only on her recognition of the shoes still adorning Addie Mae's feet.

Ms. Williams spoke vividly of the terror, anger, and hatred that sought to consume her in the years following the bombing.

I had the privilege of meeting Ms. Williams following a lecture she delivered on the campus of my alma mater, Southern Methodist University. After decades of silence, struggling with her tragic loss and fighting to maintain her sanity, she has been traveling and sharing her eyewitness account of that day. Accompanied by several youth and young adults from my church, I went, wanting them to hear Ms. Williams's story for themselves. During her lecture, Ms. Williams spoke vividly of the terror, anger, and hatred that sought to consume her in the years following the bombing. She also spoke of her Christian faith as the lifeline that sustained her will to live and as the reason she no longer carries that terror, anger, and hatred in her heart today.

During the question-and-answer period that followed her lecture, I stood to pose a question to Ms. Williams. Having organized and directed for several years an annual civil rights pilgrimage that traveled through the Deep South, I had visited many of the historic sites that she referenced in her lecture. I stated that when I had organized the pilgrimage, it was with hopes that there would be an opportunity to connect younger generations with living witnesses to this very important history—our history.

I then referred to a stone monument that has been erected in Selma, Alabama, at the foot of the Edmund Pettus Bridge. There, on March 7, 1965, six hundred peaceful marchers departed from Brown Chapel African Methodist Episcopal Church, only to be met by mounted state troopers armed with horse whips, tear gas, and cattle prods. Engraved upon the monument is a powerful imperative lifted directly from the ancient scrolls of Hebrew scripture: "When your children shall ask you in time to come, saying, 'What mean these 12 stones,' then you shall tell them how you made it over" (Josh. 4:21-22, paraphrase).

I glanced down and saw the face of my then four-year-old-son, Jeremiah, who had knelt at his seat and was playing silently near my feet. I then asked Ms. Williams what she would have my generation tell our children and future generations about her generation's experience. Without hesitation she responded, "Tell them about the great sacrifice their ancestors made to bring them to where they are today. . . . And tell them that is was God who brought us over!"

I will tell my son! And I will tell his sisters Hope and Liberty, and any more children to come. I will tell my nephew, nieces, and nephews and nieces to come, younger cousins, and cousins to come. If anyone fails to tell his or her own children, I am determined to try to tell them as well!

I will tell them that they now reap the harvest from seeds of sacrifice sown in blood, watered with sweat, and nurtured by tears. I will tell the children about a people, their people and ancestors, who—though persecuted and oppressed, marginalized and molested—propelled our nation toward true civilization and democracy. And as we reminisce together over our history, I will surely tell them about the God who brought us over!

For when we reminisce over our tumultuous past, we reminisce also over you, my God . . . the God who brought us over!

CHECK TWO

With a saddening regularity, we are losing the heroes of the American civil rights movement, leaders and foot soldiers whose fearless efforts secured for us the freedoms enjoyed by millions today. Seemingly, each week, I discover yet another post of yet another active participant in the movement who has died. And as a result, I now find within myself an even greater urgency than I have ever known to share the stories of the civil rights era with present generations and to preserve them for future generations.

Adorning the walls of my pastoral study are the pictures of such icons as Dr. Martin Luther King Jr., Rosa Parks, and Malcolm X. Also included is a picture of three young people shielding themselves from authorities who are force-spraying them with fire hoses in Birmingham, Alabama, in 1963. Emblazoned above the image of the three young people is *Courage*. Surely it took great courage to stand for justice in those days.

Truthfully, even today, it takes courage to stand up for justice in its various expressions: economic, educational, environmental, human rights, and the list goes on. The passage of time has not alleviated all destructive and oppressive forces that seek to cause harm. In reminiscing over the courage of previous generations anchored by their faith in God and in sharing these stories, I pray that we too will rise within this generation to meet the challenges of our day.

<u>CYPHER</u>

Dear God,
Help my generation rise to meet the
challenges of our day with courage and integrity.
In Jesus' name. Amen.

 <u>KEEP THE FLOW</u>

How can you keep alive the memory of the people who helped secure many of the freedoms that you enjoy today? How will you pass on their sacred witness to future generations?

PEPPER SPRAY HOSPITALITY

CHECK ONE

Good manners and common courtesy appear to be in short supply these days. They have been replaced by increasing hostilities, sometimes with deadly consequences. We have all heard reports of road rage resulting in fatalities and of guns drawn over minor and trivial disagreements. I dare argue that we are becoming a less hospitable society. On the day after Thanksgiving, known as Black Friday, this lack of hospitality is on full display. On view is not the civil rights battles where we sought and struggled and died for freedom. Rather, people are fighting for the materialistic. It truly is a dark day in our present when we see the continuing inhumanity of valuing goods above expressing goodwill toward all.

While we strive to be that idyllic nation of Thanksgiving sharing, Black Friday displays to us and the world increasing hostilities rather than hospitality.

The darkest day on the American calendar is aptly named Black Friday. No other day so vividly captures the travesty that is the American consumer culture. In recent years, Black Friday has wrought in-store fights and left dozens injured or trampled to death as crowds move into crazed hysteria in the name of big savings.

Now enter pepper spray.

Pepper spray made its Black Friday debut as one aggressive buyer, in order to secure a purchase, released the spray into a crowd of unsuspecting early morning shoppers. It's hard to compare the loss of life associated with the original Black Friday stock market catastrophe, but the pepper spray incident does create a new category for Black Friday lows: shopping by use of a lachrymal agent.

Pepper spray has been getting a lot of national coverage. We have witnessed its release upon an eighty-year-old protester, a pregnant woman, and peaceful student protesters who, while seated on the ground, were sprayed directly in their faces.

Once, as a child, I was sprayed with mace. Thankfully, it was not a direct hit; just some kids mischievously spraying into the air from the mace container attached to their mother's key ring. But then the wind shifted in my direction. It was rather unpleasant. That is an understatement. I can't imagine the pain that must be associated with a blast of pepper spray directly into one's face.

Our renewed fascination with pepper spraying one another may, in fact, reveal an unpleasantry as disturbing as our Black Friday madness. We are becoming a less hospitable nation. Any study of history would rightly reveal that hospitality has not always been best exemplified by American practice: enslaving people, violently taking land from native peoples, creating World War II concentration camps for Asians, burning down churches, burning crosses on other people's property, denying people their religious freedoms based on the extremist actions of a few, allowing generations of people to undergird US agriculture by working for next to nothing in the fields while turning a blind eye to the illegality of their presence—but now scapegoating them as the cause of drains on an economy they helped to build.

Nevertheless, it appears as though we are even more a less-hospitable nation. (Quick—name your neighbors, their kids, their dog.) Hospitality has been exchanged for a heightened hostility.

We are a spray-first-ask-questions-later society.

Let's call it pepper spray hospitality, which is, in fact, no hospitality at all.

We are a spray-first-ask-questions-later society. "I don't like your political views. Where's my pepper spray?" "I don't like your religious views. Where's my pepper spray?" "I am having a bad day, and you are in close proximity to me. Where's my pepper spray?" And I fear that, through popular media, we are passing on—as their greatest inheritance—our pepper spray hospitality to future generations.

Much of reality television programming is created to appeal to and satisfy our pepper spray delight. In great numbers, we choose to watch celebrity wives and other wealthy people—who, in great numbers, are not actually married to each other—duke it out on the small screen for our entertainment. Pepper spray hospitality at its finest! And national politics has garnered no better track record of hospitality—not with its tendency to seek to destroy rather than to work toward compromise to meet the needs of the American public.

'Tis possibly the season of pepper spray hospitality. Can anything be more heartbreaking than the story of a young woman forced to give birth to a child outdoors and surrounded by livestock, to wrap her newborn in rags, and to lay the infant in the animals' feeding trough, all because people neglected true hospitality and were unwilling to make room for her and her family indoors?

Millennia later, angels' words create for us a needed countercultural vision to our pepper spray madness: "Glory to God in the highest heaven, and on earth peace among those whom he favors" (Luke 2:14)!

CHECK TWO

Hospitality is always in season, and honey is a symbol of radical hospitality for me.

The coming of spring brought with it the usual chorus of sneezes and coughs. The visual effects of eye waterworks and athletic noses join this annual spectacle. And puffy eyes and scratchy throats star in supporting roles.

One evening as we were preparing to retire for the night, my wife, Yulise, said she was experiencing some discomfort in her throat. I arose from our bed and began my noble odyssey down the hall, through the living room, and into the kitchen, where I put some water on to boil.

I soon returned to her side with tea and an unopened economy-sized container of honey I found nestled near the back of our pantry. I could not recall buying this honey and assumed that Yulise had shopped for the sweet during one of her monthly expeditions to the food warehouse.

As I squeezed the honey into her tea, Yulise told me an anecdote that gave my rather mundane action a metaphysical quality. Unbeknownst to me, her recently deceased mother had given us the container of honey. My mother-in-law, Gloria, would often purchase items for our family during her own weekend shopping expeditions: another noisy toy or another outfit for her grandchildren.

I don't know how such a large container of honey fit into her shopping plans or what inspired the purchase. I don't know if the purchase was planned or impulsive. But what I do know is that as I squeezed out the honey into my wife's tea, I felt as though I was a conduit of a mother's love to her daughter. I could not help but think that even though my mother-in-law had been gone from us for several months, her acts of generosity and hospitality continued to flow and to minister to us.

Acts of generosity and hospitality can never be underestimated for their potential to provide strength and encouragement to others, especially when needed most. When we anticipate and then act to meet others' needs and concerns, no matter how menial, we affirm our commitment to several truths: It is better to give than to receive; we are our brother's (and sister's) keeper; and we more fully understand that "their destiny is tied up with our destiny," as Martin Luther King Jr. stated.

Where would our communities be if more people fully embraced this understanding of mutual destiny and hospitality toward others? We should all dedicate our lives to acts of radical generosity and hospitality. And we pray that these acts outlive us to encourage and support generations yet unborn.

Furthermore, our dedication to acts of radical generosity and hospitality should not be limited to people who are "just like us." We are to extend generosity and hospitality to all people, everywhere. The writer of Hebrews encourages us to "keep on loving one another as brothers and sisters. Do not forget to show hospitality to strangers, for by so doing some people have shown hospitality to angels without knowing it. Continue to remember those in prison as if you were together with them in prison, and those who are mistreated as if you yourselves were suffering" (13:1-3, TODAY'S NIV).

Regardless of persons' theology about celestial angels, the imperative contained within these words should not be overlooked. We are to extend heavenly hospitality and godlike generosity to all people!

As regal and refined as she was, my mother-in-law was also well versed in the nomenclature of the South Dallas community

31

in which she was raised. One of her favorite terms of endearment was "Honey," and she used it with great dexterity: "Honey child"; "Hon-Aye, please"; and "Hon-Aye GGGIIRRRLLL!"

To our dismay, this allergy season has caused us to return to our economy-sized container of honey several times. But on each use, I reflect on the generous spirit who provided this gift and think, *Honey, you so sweet!* And I am inspired to leave the world a little sweeter than I found it!

CYPHER

Dear God,
Help us to show radical hospitality toward each
other so that we make each other's lives sweeter.
In Jesus' name. Amen.

 **KEEP THE FLOW**

In what ways can we become more hospitable to one another? How has someone's generous act of hospitality toward you provided strength or encouragement for you?

ON COMING OF AGE
IN THE AGE OF 9/11

Acts of radical hospitality often bring with them healing, strength, and encouragement. Our hope-filled response to tragic events often yields the same, offering comfort from sorrow and community from fragmentation. Each generation faces tragedies that shape and transform its worldview. For my grandparents' generation, these were the Great Depression, the bombing of Pearl Harbor, and World War II. For my parents' generation, the tragedies included the assassinations of President John F. Kennedy, Dr. Martin Luther King Jr., and Robert Kennedy. For my generation, the greatest tragedy was the terrorist attacks against America on September 11, 2001.

As is true for many Americans, the events of 9/11 are etched in my memory. I can readily recall what I was doing when I first received word that a plane had flown into one of the Twin I was a senior in college, and my life would never be the same!

FREESTYLE

Nor would be the same my understanding of the transformative power of hope in the face of darkness.

And what do you think about all of this, Michael?" Those were the final words directed to me by NBC News anchor Tom Brokaw as I participated in a live televised interview on September 14, 2001. The interview centered on American college students' reactions to the events of 9/11. Along with my good friend and student body president, Jodi Warmbrod, I had been selected to represent Southern Methodist University during the interview. I had served as student body vice president the previous year.

Earlier that fateful week, on September 11, I had coordinated a candlelight vigil on campus. It had been a very trying week, to say the least. As the weekend approached, I had been looking forward to some needed relaxation.

After completing my last class on Friday afternoon, I walked home to my apartment, anticipating some downtime before going out that evening with friends. However, just as I crossed the threshold to my house, my cell phone rang. It was Arlene Manthey, director of student activities on campus. I needed to come to the office of public affairs at once! NBC had contacted the university, and Tom Brokaw wanted to interview college students from across the nation. A university-wide call for recommendations for two students to represent the school reportedly yielded only two names: mine and Jodi's. Hours later, I now found myself in the NBC Dallas studio, staring directly into a camera lens, an earpiece sitting uncomfortably in my right ear, with Mr. Brokaw's foreign yet familiar voice speaking to me.

After several questions to our student panel, which was representative of several other schools, including Brown University in Providence, Rhode Island, Mr. Brokaw homed in on one of my responses and immediately threw another question back to me. In questioning our panel, Mr. Brokaw had referred to my generation as the MTV generation. It seemed to suggest that we were out of touch with reality.

Mr. Brokaw openly questioned whether our generation would even be able to locate Afghanistan on the map! This assumption did not amuse me. As a political science and religious studies major who graduated a semester short of an additional major in history, I was offended by his insinuation. Confidently (maybe even defiantly) I assured him that I was well aware of current events. Mr. Brokaw then asked me to expound on my thoughts concerning the meaning of the week's events.

As I readied myself to respond, another student interrupted me, although Mr. Brokaw had addressed his question to me.

The interruption turned out to be a divine intervention that allowed me to gather my thoughts, to consider more fully the question posed. As the other student concluded his statements, Mr. Brokaw redirected without hesitation, "And, Michael, what do you think about all of this?"

I responded, "Although this is, indeed, a horrific event, our generation can restore hope. I believe we are a mighty generation . . . a generation that's quite aware that we are inheriting a world with many troubles. . . . Now we have the opportunity to make things right. I value that opportunity, and I hope to play a very important role in the future."

The hip-hop generation, the MTV generation, Generation X (take your pick), is rightly positioned to make a significant difference within our world.

Ten years later, I continue to stand behind my response. I am convinced that my generation, the hip-hop generation, the MTV generation, Generation X—take your pick—is rightly positioned to make a significant difference within our world.

I believe this because we, unlike members of other generations in recent memory, have had to overcome numerous internal obstacles to our physical, emotional, intellectual, and spiritual well-being just to make it to this point in life. We are a generation proven, tested, and committed to change.

The offspring of broken homes, we shall endeavor to keep our families together. We were largely ostracized by a church establishment that condemned us and our culture yet failed to fulfill its own core mission to "the least of these"—the sick, hungry, naked, imprisoned outsiders of present and ancient times. Our commitment to authentic spirituality "keeps it real" by placing a greater premium on what is *done* than on what is simply *spoken*.

Will change happen overnight or without struggle? Absolutely not! But having matured as young adults in the age of 9/11 and having already experienced and survived the dissolution of the "traditional" family, the decline of the church, and the disintegration of community, if there is anything that we know how to do, it is to endure despite all odds against us.

We are a mighty generation! And as our hope manifests in days to come, the world will see that what did not kill us made us stronger.

CHECK TWO

Inspired following recent travel to England in my senior year at Southern Methodist University, I was anxiously counting down the days to graduation. I was ready to begin seminary and further pursue my calling to ordained ministry.

Then planes crashed into buildings. Two towers fell. Many people died. And the world changed forever on Tuesday, September 11, 2001.

As I viewed this tragedy as it unfolded on my television screen, my internal wiring said, *Something needs to be done.* So, I did what comes naturally for an African American man shaped and nurtured by the traditions of my African American church: I put on a suit and tie and left my apartment to gather with the community. I headed to the student center. There I found a mass of students huddled in silence around television screens, struggling to make sense of what they had witnessed.

Then I headed to the administration building. It just seemed like the next thing I should do. As providence had it, when I arrived at the steps, the doors flew open and the chaplain to the university, Dr. Will Finnin, emerged. Having just left a briefing with the president, his eyes caught mine.

I proclaimed, "We need to have a candlelight vigil."

He replied, "You plan it!" as he hurried past me en route to his office to console countless students, including several from the New York area.

I immediately began planning, aided by my girlfriend (now wife). "We will need candles, lots of them, some selections from the gospel choir, words of comfort, and a moment of silence." We spent the remainder of the morning and early afternoon planning and executing. Then suddenly, I hit a wall. I had sprung into action without processing what I had seen or how it had made me feel.

Physically and emotionally drained, I sank into my chair and stared into space. After a few moments, I regained my strength and thought to myself, *I need to process this.* Then, as if I was handed something from the balconies of heaven, I sprang to my feet, endowed with new inspiration and vigor, declaring, "Journals!" We needed journals. We needed to write our thoughts and, in the process, release our emotions. As our university community gathered that evening, members did so greeted by bound journals with blank pages ready to serve as canvases for their thoughts.

A month after the terrorist attacks, I boarded a charter bus filled with students and staff from Southern Methodist University. Our student-led ministry had planned and secured funding for a community service project trip to New York City. Ours was a long, thirty-three-hour drive from Dallas to New York, but we committed to the trek to support a city that had experienced such great tragedy.

I will never forget our entry into the city. Immediately, our eyes fell upon the New York skyline. More than a month later, smoke continued to rise from the fallen towers. In such a massive city that had experienced such great loss, what could we do to make a difference? How could we spread hope? Well, since our student-led ministry was a gospel choir, we sang.

We sang in a Harlem fire station to surviving firefighters still grieving the loss of their fallen. We sang in a nursing home to elders not cognizant of the previous month's tragedies but experiencing their own grief and loss due to pain and reduced mobility. We sang upon the loading dock of an abandoned building in the South Bronx to the working poor and the homeless.

And as we sang, tears fell, not just from our listeners' eyes but from ours as well. As we sang, crowds joined in. As we sang, people clapped their hands, stomped their feet, and swayed from side to side. As we sang, we saw the glory of God! Often our singing would give invitation to prayer, and sidewalks and street corners became altars as we lifted our petitions to God.

Fast-forward ten years. I received a call from the university. The 9/11 journals, now bound into one collection, had been brought forth from the archives. Their story had caught the imagination of a dynamic young local reporter—the type you expect to see anchoring network news one day. Conducting a series of interviews on the campus, she wanted to capture my recollections of that fateful day and the journals it produced.

As I sat and viewed decade-old texts for the first time since their composition, they gripped my heart and mind. These writings were powerful and captivating. They revealed real fear, uncertainty, and anger. Yet also evident in these pages: hope.

One student wrote, "Trouble and tribulation are the greatest forces of unification." Another: "Truly this day has been one of darkness and one of light." Ten years later, dried ink upon once-blank pages presented the core emotions of life as all appeared so uncertain, and yet, there was hope in the breaking forth of a new and better day.

In reflecting about journal entries, cross-country bus rides, and gospel singing and praying with others, of this I am certain: in the midst of great tragedy, hope lives.

Hope speaks, hope journeys, hope sings, and hope prays!

CYPHER

Dear God,
Help us to restore hope in the face of tragedy,
knowing that you will give us the grace to endure.
In Jesus' name. Amen.

 **KEEP THE FLOW**

How can we restore hope for people and communities where great tragedy invades their experience and threatens their present and future? In what ways has your own experience with great difficulty or tragedy shaped your vision of a more hope-filled future?

A BANNER CALLED FREE
AT RIVERBEND
MAXIMUM SECURITY PRISON

CHECK ONE

Prison.

The mere word connotes images of barbed wire, steel bars, armed guards, and inmates locked in cells. Not hope. Not the first place that comes to mind when considering liberating and transformative experiences with God. Yet, in this least likely of places, behind prison walls, I encountered God as never before.

My prison experience with God compelled me to write so that I might share the experience with others. Not so they might encounter God vicariously through my experience, but so that this experience would inspire others to go and to encounter God for themselves in this least likely of places, a place that provided me with lessons on faith, hope, and beloved community.

A maximum security prison seems an unlikely destination when seeking a transformative encounter with God. Yet, I recently experienced God as never before amid high fences, barbed wire, legions of guards, and multiple checkpoints, while in the company of extraordinary men and women.

I attended the Fund for Theological Education's Leaders in Ministry Conference held at the historic Scarritt-Bennett Center in Nashville, Tennessee. During the conference, I participated as a roundtable leader and mentor pastor to a fresh crop of FTE Fellows as we faithfully engaged the conference theme, "Builders of Beloved Community." A site visit to the Riverbend Maximum Security Prison was part of this phenomenal experience. Over a decade past, the late Harmon Wray, Rev. Janet Wolf, and Dr. Richard Goode established a mutual learning community at Riverbend prison where students from seminaries, colleges, and congregations come to engage in theological inquiry and dialogue alongside the incarcerated.

After we successfully navigated the extensive prison checkpoints, officials escorted our group to the chapel, a small room with cinder-block walls and aged, wooden benches. When we arrived, the incarcerated persons warmly greeted us and engaged in mutual dialogue around matters of faith, rehabilitation, transformation, redemption, forgiveness, and ecclesiology. Many lessons struck me as significant during our all-too-short encounter with these amazing men.

The men spoke candidly about the failures of many prison ministries. They spoke of churches coming to Riverbend seeking only to "get them saved" but not seeking to be in community with them. They spoke of the failures of most rehabilitation practices wherein insiders learn how to regurgitate responses to the questions others pose but never undergo a true transformation of mind and spirit.

As they spoke, I could not help but think of the present-day church, which ofttimes places a greater premium on building buildings and personalities than on building transformative communities. I thought of churches that commit more to the concern of getting you "saved" than to entering into the various struggles of life with you, as well as churches more interested in what you can give rather than teaching you how to live faithfully for Christ in the world.

These men had achieved that which has proven to be a great challenge for many churches today: beloved community.

I soon recognized that within this transformative community of open dialogue and mutual sharing, these men had achieved that which has proven to be a great challenge for many churches today: *beloved community.* "Our goal is to create a beloved community and this will require a qualitative change in our souls as well as a quantitative change in our lives," wrote Martin Luther King Jr. This speaks to so much more than rehabilitation; it speaks to *transformation,* in the truest sense of that word. As the insiders spoke of how they were being made anew within this faithful community, supporting and holding one another accountable each step of the way, I witnessed hope—that we can rise above our worse selves toward the fulfillment of our better selves as never before!

None of us would glorify incarceration or the incarceration of these insiders. There is nothing glorious about prison. Some of these men committed horrific crimes that they are neither proud of nor deny. But there was something glorious about our encounter!

Inside Riverbend, people engage in theological inquiries with sincerity and urgency. Matters of forgiveness, salvation, redemption, and love are not simply fodder for intellectual enterprise but are necessities for hope and survival amid a depressing reality. Engaging theology in such a setting makes one's theology come alive. If only our theology could be as animated within our houses of worship!

I would later return to Nashville to attend the General Conference of the African Methodist Episcopal Church. Thousands of AMEs from across the world gathered to worship, fellowship, and debate; to pass legislation; and to elect denominational leadership. As I returned to this now familiar place, I did so carrying deep within me the hope of beloved community as well as a renewed commitment to help build such community at home and abroad. What better place to start than within my own Zion?

At the beginning of our dialogue with the Riverbend insiders, the persons within our circle had been invited to share what they hoped to gain from the encounter. When giving my response, I had stated, "I want to leave here transformed." As we prepared to depart after our fruitful engagement with the Riverbend insiders, a colleague noted a banner that had been hidden from sight for the duration of our encounter. I had readily taken note of three banners hanging in the chapel that read *Love*, *Hope*, and *Joy*. But I had failed to see the banner that rested just above my head, bearing the word *Free*. Though incarcerated, some since their teenage years, these transformed Riverbend men are free! They are free in the full sense of the freedom the apostle Paul articulated in his second letter to the church at Corinth. Paul penned, "Now the Lord is the Spirit, and where the Spirit of the Lord is, there is freedom" (2 Cor. 3:17). And truly, the Spirit of the Lord is at Riverbend.

I was transformed! We all were!

Now it's time to build.

CHECK TWO

Within our historic Christian witness, places of captivity have often been transformed into places of spiritual liberation and enlightenment. From the prison epistles of the apostle Paul and the powerful manifestation of the Spirit of God while Paul and Silas were in prison (the book of Acts), to the vision of heaven that John had while imprisoned on the Isle of Patmos, God has shown Godself mighty, even behind prison walls.

Even within our modern Christian heritage, prison, as unlikely as it may seem, has emerged as a place of liberation in

God. Some fifty years ago, over the Easter weekend of 1963, Dr. Martin Luther King Jr. sat in solitary confinement, having been arrested in the city of Birmingham, Alabama, for his participation in Birmingham's justice campaign for nonviolence named Project C. During his confinement, several clergypersons published an article in a local newspaper, chiding King for his actions. They wrote in summation, "We recognize the natural impatience of people who feel their hopes are slow in being realized. But we are convinced that these demonstrations are unwise and untimely."

In response to their letter, King penned one of the greatest nonviolent treatises and defenses of a social movement in human history, simply titled "Letter from Birmingham Jail." Upon scraps of paper smuggled to him by a Negro jail trustee and around the margins of that very newspaper condemning his work, King etched into the annals of history such monumental truths as, "Injustice anywhere is a threat to justice everywhere" and "Freedom is never voluntarily given by the oppressor; it must be demanded by the oppressed."

The letter would become the crown jewel of *Why We Can't Wait*, a book King published the next year. The prevailing spirit of this text could not be stated with more perfect simplicity as King argued, "Justice too long delayed is justice denied." Although it was King who was incarcerated, it is clear to history that King was freer in God than the clergypersons who authored their ill-advised letter condemning his work, his commitment to justice.

While I do not advocate comprehensive prison terms for all people seeking God, it bears consideration that when Jesus addressed his disciples, he included prison as a place of faithful encounters with God. Jesus spoke to his disciples, "I needed clothes and you clothed me, I was sick and you looked after me, I was in prison and you came to visit me" (Matt. 25:36, TODAY'S

NIV). Clearly, Jesus knew that prison spaces could make for powerful spiritual engagement. It would do the church well to revisit how we engage prisons' insiders, for this offers much more to the church than opportunities for prison evangelistic ministry. Insiders offer the church a vision of the beloved community that Christ has called the church to become.

CYPHER

Dear God,
Help us to have more liberating and transformative
encounters with you in more of what we misguidedly perceive
as the least likely spaces for such encounters.
In Jesus' name. Amen.

 **KEEP THE FLOW**

What is the least likely place that you have had a transformative experience with God? How can the church minister to those who are incarcerated?

AN UNEXPECTED ENCOUNTER WITH HUMAN EXCREMENT

CHECK ONE

Ministry, as with life, is filled with serendipitous moments. Better stated, these are not chance. Rather, they are providential moments that move beyond rationalization, moments both captivating and awe inspiring, even though unusual. Never would I have imagined that one of my most important lessons in ministry would transpire next to a garbage bin. And never would I have imagined that it would involve human feces.

But it did! And I am the better for having had the experience. Yet truthfully, I almost missed the moment. Initially I allowed disgust and frustration to blind me to the reality of human suffering. There is no way to separate human feces from humanity; this encounter allowed me to see humanity and the nature of human suffering more clearly than I had ever seen before.

FREESTYLE

Reflecting compelled me to write. I hope people will not miss what I came conspicuously close to missing: No matter how initially off-putting, all human suffering deserves a witness.

Last Sunday, I encountered an unusual blessing: human excrement adorning the cold pavement. I did not, however, initially receive it as the great blessing that it was.

As I arrived at church early Sunday morning, I noticed that our dumpster had been disturbed. This is not unusual for those of us engaging in ministry in urban contexts. I assumed that a homeless person had come and searched our dumpster overnight for food.

As I approached the dumpster to secure it, I noticed a single, stained, white sock resting on the ground. The sock was surrounded by several translucent, dial-shaped entities. A closer look revealed them to be pieces of dead skin, likely peeled from a human foot. I suddenly recalled reading that homeless people walk upward of thirteen miles a day. Undoubtedly, their feet are covered with calluses, bruises, and blisters.

Then I saw them, in the corner of our gated waste-disposal area—two pieces of human waste lying conspicuously on the ground.

This unexpected encounter ushered me through a range of emotions. My first, disgust! While well acquainted with excrement, most notably my own and that encountered through diaper changing, I am not accustomed to encountering items such as these outside my home, much less in such a public space.

Then I felt frustrated! The feces could not be ignored. Though silent, their presence screamed at me! I had to address the situation. And it would have been irresponsible for me to wait for others to tend to it. I had to handle this matter myself.

I was also insulted! Who would dare defecate on someone else's property, let alone church property? *Have they no respect for themselves? Have they no respect for the house of God?*

With these emotions bubbling over, I entered the church. After retrieving some plastic bags, I returned and knelt down to remove the excrement. My now close encounter with the matter at hand provided me with greater insight into its former carrier. While I am no medical expert, some truths were immediately discernible through my brief observation.

On account of its discoloration, it appeared sickly and diseased. Something was obviously awry with the carrier's digestive system. It also appeared painful. Streaks of blood painted its exterior. At the risk of assigning anthropomorphic qualities to human waste, it appeared lonely and rejected. It might have gone unnoticed except for our encounter.

I disposed of the matter and returned to the church to prepare for worship. That Sunday we had a powerful day of worship in both the morning and the afternoon. Confessions of faith were made, new members united with our worship community, and many left empowered to serve. After the day's services, I returned to my study to reflect on the day's events. While there, I recalled the feces vividly. And as I did, I found myself first convicted—and then blessed.

Too often the church is quick to meet human suffering with disgust and frustration rather than compassion and service.

Too often the church, as I did, first encounters human suffering, or the evidence of human suffering, with the wrong set of emotions. Too often the church is, as I was, quick to meet human suffering with disgust and frustration rather than compassion and service. And far too often, the church perceives certain activity as an insult rather than what it truly is: a cry for help.

The church should never turn away from those seeking relief from the pains of life, no matter how undesirable the cause of their pain. When Jesus encountered ten men suffering from leprosy, he did not turn away. When

Jesus encountered a woman suffering from continuous vaginal bleeding, he did not turn away. Jesus always had time for the sick, the hurting, the hungry, the poor, and the dying. Jesus desired the undesirable, the rejected, those who found themselves lying on life's cold pavement in silence, whose presence and suffering screamed for notice.

Even in the midst of our urban setting, where human suffering surrounds us daily and despite our young church's commitment to community empowerment, my encounter was a needed and powerful reminder that human suffering is ever present. And as a church, we seek to eliminate human suffering whenever, wherever, and however possible.

While I am not rushing toward another public encounter with human waste, on this occasion I did ultimately find hope in this experience. It became an odd consolation for me that the carrier found relief, albeit temporary, from what obviously had pained him or her along an undoubtedly uncomfortable journey. And I was gifted by God with the blessed opportunity to receive and dispose of it. Thus, while the person may have gone unseen, his or her suffering did not go unnoticed.

While in my study, I offered a prayer for a still-unknown visitor that Sunday. I also offered a prayer for myself. I prayed never to turn away from human need or become detached from human suffering. No matter how it is expressed, no matter in what form it is encountered.

I invite your prayers as well!

CHECK TWO

Over the course of the next decade, my generation will rise to lay claim to greater positions of power and authority, influence, and responsibility throughout society. However, I have deep concerns that if my generation does not properly address the demons of our childhood, we are doomed either to repeat the mistakes of our parents' generation or to be stagnant because of those mistakes in the years to come. And this would prove most tragic, not only for our society but for our world as a whole.

The prominent issues that confront my generation are great in multitude and potent in impact. The issues range from paternal absenteeism, which I, like many, deem to be society's greatest ill, to the AIDS epidemic that emerged during my childhood. Yet, another issue has not often been given its proper due, one that I have confronted several times in ministry. This issue in part also defines my generation. We are the children of *addiction*. And the children of addiction are suffering in silence.

Certainly addiction, particularly substance abuse, did not originate with my parents' generation. Previous generations have known well the grim perils associated with parental addiction. But I argue that in previous generations this addiction was not as widespread. The rise of heroin, cocaine, crack-cocaine, methamphetamines, even alcohol abuse over the last thirty years, has had dire consequences on an entire generation. In many cases, the children of addiction were robbed of their childhood and forced to grow up all too fast.

The children of addiction lead lives of incredible hardship. From an early age, these children are taught, even forced in many cases, to veil their parents' addiction from the public eye. They learn how to cover for their parents' absence from work or erratic behavior while in public. Even before reaching driving age, they are well acquainted with the need to drive inebriated, "stoned," and passed-out parents home. These children have held their parents' heads steady over toilets. Theirs has been the great misfortune of cleaning parents soiled by their own vomit, blood, urine, and feces. They have gazed at parents through plates of prison glass over countless holidays. In too many earth-shattering cases, the children of addiction have been the first to discover a parent's lifeless body and to make arrangements for burial after an overdose.

The tragedy of addiction transcends classifications and labels. I have witnessed its impact on former high school classmates from the impoverished Bottoms of Third Ward to the mansions of River Oaks in Houston, Texas. From the hardened streets of South Dallas to the manicured lawns of Highland Park, near where I attended college, I have witnessed such addiction passed on as an inheritance to an emerging generation.

In my pastoral ministry, now rapidly approaching its tenth anniversary as I write, I have engaged countless parishioners who are the children of addiction. Even now, as young adults—some with children of their own—the pain of their parents' addiction remains present with them and continues to manifest itself within them as shame and distrust of others. As adults, some still seek to provide cover for parents struggling with addiction.

Our church has provided support and outreach to both church members and community neighbors gripped by addiction. Many of them are parents who have wept openly, lamenting their separation from their children. And yet many would choose their next high over being reunited with their children; the disease of addiction is too strong a shackle to break without greater assistance.

That aforementioned excrement was more than just excrement. For me, the waste became a symbol of human suffering; I could not help but think, *How many more people, especially children, are suffering because of its former carrier's absence?*

<u>CYPHER</u>

Dear God,
Increase my awareness of human suffering,
that I not miss the opportunity to bear witness to the pain.
Strengthen my stamina to provide relief to those
I encounter who suffer each day.
In Jesus' name. Amen.

 KEEP THE FLOW

In what ways do you see people suffering? How might you engage them in order to provide needed relief? If you are suffering from your own addictions or those of someone close to you, how can others support you and encourage you to reach out for help?

PART TWO

FAMILY

FAMILY

When I think of family, I think of Christmas as a child. My family would often gather at my grandparents' home in Marlin, Texas. For my grandmother Naomi, the house was her canvas. Her decorating talents were on display in every room. Leaving the main food preparation to my grandmother, my grandfather Bishop could always be counted on for his signature smoked turkey.

My mother, Brenda, was the family's "official" gift wrapper and coordinator of family traditions. She ensured that the annual reading of Jesus' birth narrative always transpired before opening gifts. My uncle Willis traveled the farthest and arrived last; but once he arrived you knew it, for he always brought his outgoing personality with him.

I, the roamer, wanted to be a part of everything. I would roam into the kitchen, where my grandmother was cooking, for a sample. This often backfired, and she would draft me to assist in food preparation. Once freed from the kitchen, I would roam outside where my grandfather was smoking the bird on the pit. My grandfather, the storyteller, would recount days long past. He painted such vivid pictures with his words that each person, location, and scene came to life.

I would roam back inside as my mother was wrapping gifts. She would also draft me, but the excitement of knowing each person's gift made it worth the effort. I shadowed my uncle when he arrived. My playful uncle would quickly toss me in the air.

The highlight of Christmas was the impromptu musical that transformed the house into a sanctuary. Bishop would get on the piano and play hymns. Brenda would begin to sing, ultimately making her way to accompany Bishop on the organ.

My mother and grandfather continued to play and sing until Willis arrived. My grandfather would proudly vacate the piano and listen to my mother and uncle play together. Naomi would be content in the kitchen until a song moved her spirit. Then she would make her grand entrance, singing in her pure soprano voice.

With the entire family assembled, the singing continued until my mother got "happy." My grandfather, laughing with joy, repeating again and again, "All right! All right!" My grandmother shedding tears, and my uncle lifting us higher in praise.

All the while I sat there with just my eyes roaming now, a smile on my face. This was my family, and I knew that what we had was special.

SHE LOVES ME ("YULISE" IN E-FLAT)

CHECK ONE

My wife and I have often debated concerning the first time we met. It really is not much of a debate. As with most things, she is right. Our first meeting came at the end of an orientation-week student forum with upperclassmen, when we were freshmen entering college. The adviser to African American students called the two of us together and stated that we would be her "freshmen babies" that year.

The problem is that I don't remember our meeting. I entered that student forum petrified, having sprinted across campus in an attempt to attend a portion of the forum before it adjourned. I had been in the financial aid office for most of the morning, waiting in agony to finalize the monies needed for my tuition—in agony because I was missing the most important meeting of a college career that had not yet officially begun. I finally arrived, so flustered that all I remember is making a joke that garnered hefty laughter: "Where can a brother get something to eat around here?"

However, I have no trouble remembering the first time I beheld Yulise. It was August 23, 1998, the day before the start of classes. We were in Selecman Hall, attending the first rehearsal of the year for the Voices of Inspiration Gospel Choir. I stood in the center with the tenors, getting to know the men in my section. I happened to look to my left toward the soprano section where a ray of sunlight beamed through the western-facing windows as the sun began to make its descent. I followed that ray until it shone on the bright, dimpled smile of Yulise.

And for a moment, I wondered if it was her smile and not the sun that had created such radiance in our rehearsal. It would be an entire year before we would kindle our relationship, yet I can never forget the first time I "officially" laid eyes on my wife.

This experience is only trumped by the first time I laid eyes on her six years later as she walked to meet me at the altar at our wedding. On the occasion of our wedding anniversary, I reflected anew on our special day, as well as all that we had experienced in life and in love since.

One glorious Saturday morning, I stood at the foot of the hallowed altar of a stunningly beautiful chapel. I was donned in tails, anxiously peering down a seemingly endless aisle, greatly anticipating the swinging open of towering doors and the grand entrance of my bride. Today my memory recalls many snapshots of that day. The light of the sun dancing through windowpanes. Her long train gathering rose petals like railcars to accompany her as she made a long walk to join me at the altar. The fresh paint of manicured toes peeking forth from beneath the hem of her wedding dress, noticeable to me on each downward glance for prayer. Streaming tears inconspicuously cloaked by a veil. My tears, which were not. A shout of praise at the glory of the day. Our kiss.

Years later, anxious anticipation of her appearance has yet to cease. Mine is the daily anticipation of crossing the threshold of our abode to the greeting of her warm embrace. Mine is the daily gift of her effervescent personality empowered by her engaging smile, her tender touch, her bountiful beauty. When I am away from her presence, mine too is the anxious anticipation of her texts, e-mails, or calls to say, "I love you!"

Our marriage is being perfected
with each passing day.

While we rightly and roundly enjoy the fruits of our physical intimacy, given to us as a sacred trust by God, our greater intimacy transcends human touch. As husband and wife, we openly share our dreams, our hopes, our fears, and our struggles. We anticipate each other's needs, fiercely guard each other's heart, rejoice in each other's successes, and stand unwaveringly by each other's side when we meet with disappointment.

Who could have imagined that the woman I had mistaken for an upper-classman on our first encounter as freshmen, due to her striking confidence and poise, would become my wife, the mother of our glorious children, my life partner, and my best friend? Surely, God above! Surely, the angels in heaven! For Yulise is one of their own! Yulise is proof positive that angels exist and that they sometimes walk on the earth. In all ways possible, she not only completes me but makes me a better me.

Our marriage is not perfect. No marriage is. We consider our union to be beautifully human—in some places strong, in others weak. But we feel confident that our marriage is being perfected with each passing day. Our human experience has dealt us a plethora of life experiences. We have laughed together, cried together, rejoiced in birthing rooms, consoled each other near headstones, and loved each other with imperfect human perfection.

As a pastor, I have been blessed to lead numerous couples in exchanging marital vows. A family law attorney, my wife has aided numerous clients along the path toward marital dissolution. Together, our professional experiences also make us aware of the sacredness of our union, that what we have is special, and how quickly it can all be lost if not given proper care and attention. Therefore, we choose to live life like it's golden, being quick to forgive, slow to get angry, and purposeful in our communication with each other.

During preaching in the African American tradition, musicians often accompany the sermon's crescendo with a melodic interchange. It makes for a harmonious arrangement of words and sounds. Within this tradition is the recitation of a sacred hymn during the crescendo. At my preaching's height, I crescendo in the key of E-flat.

Therefore, as I now reach the crescendo of this ode to my bride upon our anniversary, I do so by reciting a few words from a sacred hymn composed by the psalmist Jill Scott, that I adapted for my bride:

"Yulise loves me! She keeps me on my feet happily excited by her perfume, her hands, her smile, her intelligence."

And I will forever love you!

CHECK TWO

My wife and I share a wedding anniversary with my maternal grandparents. Bishop and Naomi were married for sixty years before my grandfather's death. At our wedding reception, Yulise and I presented my grandparents with an anniversary cake for their fifty-fifth.

Theirs was a lifetime of love and was not always easy.

Bishop was a gifted pianist, and while he was in college, he would play in jazz bands for additional income. He would often send much of that money home to his mother to help her make ends meet and to support her ministry. Bishop's mother, Willie B., was one of the first female pastors in Texas.

Bishop loved jazz music in part because it is a complex genre of music with interchanging major and minor chords, ever increasing and decreasing tempos, and improvisation. The jazz genre is also known for its effective use of "blue notes." A blue note, as defined in *Wikipedia*, is "a note sung or played at a lower pitch than that of the major scale, for expressive purposes." As such, I believe that jazz music is a metaphor for life itself: beautifully complex, ever-changing tempos, and blue notes.

For me, the blue notes of life are those low points of life, those difficult and trying seasons of life, those times of heartache and hardship that we all experience. We discover blue notes scattered across the music scales of our lives. Jesus promised the presence of blue notes when he said, "I have said this to you, so that in me you may have peace. In the world you face persecution. But take courage; I have conquered the world!" (John 16:33).

If blue notes are an inescapable part of life, we must pose the question, "How do we handle the blue notes of our lives?"

There were several blue-note moments in Bishop and Naomi's marriage. When Bishop and Naomi lost their first child at childbirth. When Bishop and Naomi both suddenly lost siblings who were young adults. And when Bishop was diagnosed with an incurable cancer and placed in hospice care. Blue notes.

But for sixty years, they never faced a blue note alone.

And Yulise and I have discovered in our own marriage that this truth is what makes for a successful marriage. It's not the absence of challenge or difficulty, the avoidance of blue-note moments—but a love that grows stronger in the face of these notes that blesses a married couple. It is a blessing to know that you will never have to face these moments alone.

CYPHER

Dear God,
Help us in marriage to grow stronger in our unions,
knowing that, even in the face of blue-note moments,
we have been blessed with the opportunity to face them together.
In Jesus' name. Amen.

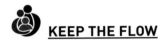 **KEEP THE FLOW**

What married couple has inspired you? In what ways can communities nurture and support married couples who are experiencing "blue-note" moments in their marriage? What are the blue notes in your relationship, and how have you overcome them?

GLORY
A NEW DAY FOR FAMILY AND FATHERHOOD IN HIP-HOP CULTURE

<u>CHECK ONE</u>

The birth of a child is a significant event in family life. It is a cause for celebration, for elation, for jubilation! However, in far too many cases for present generations, fathers have not been present to take part in these special moments. So when a father is present to welcome his child into the world, it is a noteworthy event. There are probably no more celebrated new parents in the world at this writing than Beyoncé and Shawn Carter, better known as Jay-Z, his rap pseudonym.

The world greatly anticipated their firstborn child. I marveled at what the birth of this child to Jay-Z meant for family and fatherhood in the age of hip-hop culture and how it might inspire present and future fathers to step up to the plate.

One of the most highly anticipated births in recent memory has now taken place. The first child of Jay-Z and Beyoncé Knowles, a daughter, Blue Ivy Carter, entered the world weighing seven pounds on Saturday, January 7, 2012, at a New York hospital. I pray God's continued blessings on the family.

In honor of his firstborn, Jay-Z quickly recorded and released a masterful song, "Glory." The song has the potential of becoming this generation's "Isn't She Lovely?," Stevie Wonder's tribute to his newborn daughter, Aisha, from the classic album *Songs in the Key of Life* (1976). I identify with such creative inspiration and the immediate need for expression. In the week leading up to the birth of my first child, I preached a sermon inspired by the meaning of that anticipated birth. I preached likewise about each successive child's birth. The overwhelming joy of fatherhood is its own inspiration, but I now find inspiration for expression in Jay-Z's "Glory."

When Beyoncé rubbed her belly after a dynamic performance at the MTV Music Awards and the camera then shot to an ecstatic Jay-Z flashing a 1,000-watt smile, I believed it to be one of the most important popular culture moments of this century. Sadly, popular media rarely capture a happily married African American family basking in the glow of the anticipated birth of a child. It is tragic, to say the least, that the number of children born out of wedlock is increasing in America in general and within the African American community specifically, where 70 percent of African American children are born outside of the marriage covenant.

Such attempts to redefine family *trouble me deeply.*

I am aware that my expressed concerns place me at odds with some. I am among a fleeting number of individuals who believe that God's plan is for children to be born within the confines of a marital union. Nonetheless, I believe.

Honestly, I hoped that my generation, the hip-hop generation (or Generation X), deeply scarred by the absence of our own fathers, would not repeat our fathers' mistakes. Increasingly, I see my hopes dashed. While the celebration of the sacrament of baptism was moving and the family members supportive—as a pastor concerned for family, I recently came to a grim realization. Of the last fifteen children I have baptized, only four fathers had been present for the celebration of the sacrament. Of those fathers present, only one father was married to the woman with whom the child was conceived. And for me, it appears as if the trend of fatherless baptisms will continue in the near future.

Yes, I know that my concerns are at odds, especially with those who actively advocate for the redefinition of the family. Such attempts to redefine *family* trouble me deeply. Redefinition of family formerly came due to necessity, such as after tragedy or disappointment; after a failed marriage; incarceration; a parent with a substance abuse problem; or even the death of one or both parents, which resulted in other family members or friends stepping in to raise the children. Today, many families redefine at the point of conception, as marriage is no longer considered a prerequisite to beginning a family.

I applaud Jay-Z and Beyoncé for accomplishing what many in my generation have failed to do: breaking the cycle of absenteeism established by their parents' generation. Jay-Z's dedication to breaking this cycle is vividly captured in his recent recordings. In the song "New Day" from Jay-Z and Kanye West's *Watch the Throne*, Jay-Z raps, "Promise to never leave him . . . 'cause my dad left me and I promise [to] never repeat him." Such important reflections on the meaning of fatherhood and commitment to the next generation are diminishing within our society.

Admittedly, I did not see this coming. After years of listening to Jay-Z spit verses about material opulence, drug-dealing escapades, and womanizing, the possibility never entered my mind that one day he would be revered as a husband and a father. Popular hip-hop has never been known as a bastion of morality or familial commitment. Yet, these recent reflections on fatherhood from perhaps the genre's most recognized living artist could signify a new day for fatherhood, accountability, and responsibility expressed not only within the genre but throughout the culture. And because of the tremendous influence of hip-hop culture on American society, I pray that it might also serve as a new day for the reclamation of the importance of fatherhood, accountability, and responsibility throughout America.

With hope and anticipation of such reclamation of family and fatherhood in American society, there is only one possible response:

Glory!

CHECK TWO

On July 4, 2013, Jay-Z released his highly anticipated twelfth studio album, *Magna Carta Holy Grail.* Of the many themes engaged on this album, I find Jay-Z's reflections on fatherhood most intriguing. Here Jay-Z exposes his deep feelings of inadequacy as a father.

Jay-Z notes that fatherhood can be both a joyful and a frightening experience. This is especially true for a generation born to largely absent fathers. In a video marketing the album, Jay-Z joyfully acknowledges that Blue is "something that [they] both created. We still marvel at her." Then suddenly Jay-Z bemoans his own father's abandonment of him, stating that his father never taught him how to be a man, how to raise a child, or how to treat a woman. Jay-Z acknowledges that he desperately needs those lessons now and offers as a summary statement,

"It's the paranoia of not being a great dad."

In lyrics from "Jay-Z Blue," Jay-Z reveals that he remains haunted by his father's failures and the dissolution of his parents' troubled marriage. I, like many young fathers today, many of whom are the products of absent fathers and failed marriages, can identify with Jay-Z's joy and pain. Upon holding each of my children for the first time, I vividly recall becoming the embodiment of complex dualities: strength and weakness, assurance and fear, confidence and self-doubt each simultaneously encompassing my being.

As a collective work, Jay-Z's offering appears more theological than others. There is nothing like fatherhood to make a person more intimately aware of God's presence. Yet, even in the presence of God, feelings of inadequacy can remain. Such was the case for me. On my son's fourth birthday, I bemoaned the fact that our four short years together had exceeded the entirety of my experience growing up with my father. And I too began to question whether or not I had what it took to raise my son.

There is a clear and present danger in the emotions that Jay-Z, I, and many young fathers have shared. These emotions can cause us to overcompensate for what we lacked in a father and to subject ourselves to the self-imposed pressure and unattainable feat of being the "perfect" father. Too many fathers have been guilty of viewing fatherhood as perfection.

Thankfully, in the face of fears and feelings of inadequacy, Jay-Z acknowledges his frailty by rapping on "Jay-Z Blue," "I know I'm not perfect, baby." This revelation comes as a gift to us all, for in it we can find the liberation to be the best fathers that we can be without being haunted by the past or fearful of the future. It is the revelation that our greatest ambition as fathers should not be perfection but being a loving, faithful, and consistent presence in our children's lives.

It is exceedingly more important for our children to know that their fathers love them and are present for them than for fathers to cling to the farce that unattainable perfection is the goal. Once liberated to pursue faithfulness over perfection, prayerfully, a new generation of fathers will find an independence day of their own, free from the past and inspired by the hope of a greater future.

CYPHER

Dear God,
Help us as fathers to provide love, nurture,
and support to our children so that they will grow strong
and emerge in life as productive citizens and effective workers
in your kingdom.
In Jesus' name. Amen.

 **KEEP THE FLOW**

What resources and support systems are available in your community for persons who seek healing from childhood trauma? How can your community support and encourage new fathers who are healing from their own father-less experience? Who do you identify as your father figure, and how have you allowed that person to have a place in your life? If you've experienced brokenness in your relationship with your father, whether you are a son or a daughter, in what ways does your heavenly Father help?

PRETTY GIRL ROCK

<u>CHECK ONE</u>

Without question, my middle child is the bravest person I know. She has had a lifetime of medical procedures in her short four years of life. She has a rather intimate knowledge of chest tubes and IVs, along with the beeps of machines measuring every function of her body. She is as strong as a rock, and her body's scars testify to her experience.

I must admit that despite her bravery, as her father I am compelled to ensure that she in no way feels deficient or inferior because of her unique experience or because of her scars. This is not a simple task to take on within our society. For a long time, people—especially women and young girls—have been held up to impossible standards of beauty. Oftentimes, they have been pressured to attain the unattainable in order to gain acceptance based almost exclusively on how they look rather than the persons they are. Given the innumerable pressures to reach a standard of beauty that has been faced by women who have experienced far less than my girl, I quickly began to contemplate my role as her father to shield her against such hurtful expectations.

Thankfully, my chance encounters of self-discovery with my daughter at our hallway mirror provided me with both the inspiration and the opportunity to protect her from these pressures as well as to uplift her impeccable beauty. I hope that our experience will help others as they attempt to shield and uplift their daughters as well.

I will never forget the moment I saw my daughter's heart beating inside her chest. Several months before her birth, during a prenatal visit to the doctor's office, our nurse furrowed her brow as she studied pictures of the sonogram. She hurriedly departed to get the doctor. As he studied the sonogram, his brow furrowed too.

Something was wrong. We were referred immediately to a pediatric cardiologist. The cardiologist gave us a name for our daughter's condition: *hypoplastic left heart syndrome*. Our daughter's heart had not fully developed all of its chambers. To correct it, she would need three life-saving, open-heart surgeries—one within the first week of life, the second within her first six months, and the third somewhere around three years.

So there we stood, my wife and I, four days after our daughter's birth—surrounded by surgeons and nurses, many whose brows furrowed, others who could not look us in our eyes, at least two who quickly ducked out of the room to avoid our noticing tears in theirs—looking down on our daughter as she lay motionless, her mouth ajar, her chest cavity opened, her beating heart visible through a protective film stitched into her skin. They did not expect her to survive the night. But she did! That night, and the next, and 724 nights since, and counting!

As my wife and I looked over her, I vividly remember the first words that came forth from my mouth: "Hey, pretty girl!" Only recently has my use of this salutation arisen with greater meaning within my consciousness. "Hey, pretty girl!" It has been my morning greeting to her for nearly her entire life. I have discovered myself repeatedly speaking these words to her throughout the day, "Hey, pretty girl!"

She looked up toward me, then back toward the mirror, and spoke with a deep conviction and knowledge of her own essence, "Pretty girl."

A few months ago, our daughter discovered her reflection in our full-length hallway mirror. Every day since, she pauses to look at herself and study her reflection. She does so not with vanity but with a pure curiosity that ultimately turns to play. And as she engages in this daily ritual, I walk up beside her and say, "Hey, pretty girl!" Then she giggles and smiles—and my heart melts. Two weeks ago, a stunning new development occurred. When I walked up to her and said, "Hey, pretty girl," she looked up toward me, then back toward the mirror, and spoke with a deep conviction and knowledge of her own essence, "Pretty girl."

Our daughter has grown to become a determined, strong-minded, opinionated, confident, ultra-cute little girl. She is a fighter, and, undoubtedly, she has needed every ounce of fight within her to make it this far. Through no shortage of miracles, she survived her first and second surgeries despite major complications with both. You would not know the gravity of her experience by looking at her.

Not unless you see her scars.

Although I have changed her diapers, and bathed, lotioned, and dressed her, the scars still give me pause. They cause me to remember the beating heart behind them all over again. As she grows toward greater self-awareness, as evidenced by the increasing frequency of visits to the hallway mirror, I have begun to anticipate the day when she inquires, "What do these scars mean? Where did they come from?"

My preparation for that day has made me even more conscious of how miserably oppressive our culture is when it objectifies women's bodies. Our daughters daily walk through a maze of profit-driven images bombarding them with superficial, fictitious standards of beauty. The result can be tragic and deadly. Seeking to *be* the standards, wanting that "beauty" that's peering at them from magazine covers to music videos, millions of women succumb to plastic surgery, suffer from bulimia, become anorexic, and more.

I recognize that I, as her father, am my daughter's first line of defense against such bombardment.

I must defend her, both now and in the future, against anything and anybody that would seek to degrade her scar-laden body as though her imperfections are undesirable. I am to affirm her inner and outer beauty, her strength, her gifts, and the promise of her future. I must let her know that her scars are beautiful! And they tell a powerful story. Her scars are reminders of the care rendered by skilled and able hands. Without those scars, there would be no life to celebrate. And life, even life best exemplified through scar tissue, is beautiful! She is made pretty, not in the absence of scars but because of them.

One day I will have to let her go: to college, to vocation, to love. But even then, she will be my pretty girl. And with strength and determination as solid as a rock, she will face any future challenges or obstacles that may stand in her way with the same determination with which she has faced these early ones, scars and all.

For now, I will enjoy our daily ritual play by the mirror. Every time we meet at her reflected image, I will declare, "Hey, pretty girl!"

I will hear her respond in kind.

Pretty girl, rock on!

CHECK TWO

My daughter recently had the final open-heart surgery in a triad of surgeries. By the grace of God, she recovered well in the hospital and was released to continue her recovery at home. While we have been able to remove some of the bandages that were on her arm, some of the bandages on her chest remain as I write, and they are to remain until such time as they peel and come off by themselves.

I am cognizant of the fact that beneath those bandages are scars that are still healing. And while her gifted and able doctors worked diligently to reduce the visibility of those scars for the long term, for a season those scars will be readily visible to everyone, including my daughter. Leading up to her final surgery, my daughter began to relate to her scars with a level of intrigue and mystery. She had always had the scars, and she knew they were from her previous surgeries; but since she was too young at the time of those surgeries to process what had happened to her, though she knew the scars, she did not know the pain.

I pray that innocence will remain: of knowing the scars but not the pain. I mean this not in the sense that she will not experience physical pain, for with her recent surgery, she already has. But this is to say that she will not experience another kind of pain that far too many of our daughters and their mothers have experienced: the pain of trying to live up to an unreasonable standard of beauty that devalues the beauty they possess within.

<u>CYPHER</u>

Dear God,
Help us to see that we are much more than our scars.
You have made us far too complex to be defined by what is without
as opposed to what is within. Forgive us for the times when we have
devalued ourselves, as well as for the times when we have devalued others,
for as the psalmist wrote in lyric, "I praise you, for I am fearfully
and wonderfully made. Wonderful are your works; that I know very well"
(Ps. 139:14).
In Jesus' name. Amen.

 ## <u>KEEP THE FLOW</u>

What can you do to counter the bombardment of superficial standards of beauty and their negative impact on the psyche of young people? What "scars" do you possess that you must begin to celebrate or find beauty in?

A PAINFUL (YET FAMILIAR) RITUAL

CHECK ONE

Looking at my wife, Yulise, seated comfortably on the passenger side of the car during a recent family road trip, I had a flashback. I saw in her place myself, seated in Papa Bishop's pickup. And I recall how he drove down country roads and wove stories of his past into my future. He taught me about hazards familiar to him yet undiscovered by me. Once I thought we were lost on what seemed an endless road going nowhere. Papa finally made a sharp left turn and before us stood a massive tree with strong branches jutting out. It towered above us in the middle of the road, splitting it into two forks. Papa chose one and drove further, got out, and questioned a man while pointing back in the direction of the tree. Papa had been elected county road commissioner. "Is that the hanging tree?"

The man, looking down in shame, uttered, "Yes."

Papa's words often stretched my life and broadened my understanding, taking me on a journey to understand faith and family and more, including justice, which is part and parcel to our families' survival.

I must admit that I arrived at the story of Troy Anthony Davis rather late. I had seen his picture in various articles as well as posted on social media groups for years. I was aware of the movement in Georgia to spare his life from capital punishment, but I had not followed the progress of this movement closely. It was not until the final weeks of his life approached and the news cycle began repeating his story that I began to pay more attention to it. And also to the numerous and heralded individuals who were speaking out against his intended execution, claiming that there was insufficient evidence that he committed murder.

On the day of the scheduled execution, I watched the evening news from my barber's chair, hoping and praying for a stay of execution. Having watched and read many reports over the past several weeks, I was convinced that Troy Anthony Davis's case deserved to be reconsidered. An attorney in my Facebook friends' list prematurely posted that a stay of execution had been offered. I was cautiously optimistic. Sadly, a stay was not extended.

Once our family arrived home for the evening and settled in, I turned on the news to continue watching coverage of the approaching execution. Some reporters began questioning the validity of the capital charges. Notable dignitaries, from former US President Jimmy Carter to retired Anglican Archbishop Desmond Tutu, spoke out in support of a stay of execution. Their efforts were unsuccessful.

PART TWO: FAMILY

The news soon reported that Troy Anthony Davis was dead. Davis's death surfaced many thoughts in me. *How could such a major public outcry and the voiced protests of such international dignitaries not result in a reconsideration of the case?* My thoughts and feelings intensified as I gazed down at my son, who had been playing on the floor in front of the television the entire time, oblivious to the fate playing out on the screen before him. And as I looked on at my son and then at the images on the screen, my emotions bubbled over, and I contemplated what it means to be a Black man in America. I then became painfully aware that I would have to discuss this topic with my son, sooner rather than later. I would have to begin etching away at his blissful innocence, for this was a discussion I recalled the elders in my family had with me when I was a youth. The discussion was sure to be painful yet so familiar.

At this writing, my only son turned five years old last week. He is a handsome, articulate, energetic, intelligent, fun-loving, and gentle young man. He is the apple of my eye! There's only one problem in America's view; he is *Black*.

And as his father, I am challenged to do for him what generations of African American fathers have had to do for their sons for far too long in this country; I must inform him that because of his unique blend of gender and pigmentation, he must contend with a different set of rules while growing up.

Nineteen years ago, on a frigid December night in Waco, Texas, what was intended to be a quick stop at the convenience store turned into a two-hour lesson on the racial history of America. I was a teenager wearing a large jacket with a hood. As I readied myself to exit the car, my grandfather, whom we were visiting for the holidays, proclaimed, "Take that hood off your head before you go in that store, or they will blow your brains out!" Such sudden outbursts were uncharacteristic for my rather mild-mannered grandfather.

His proclamation of the possibility of my abrupt and violent end upset me. And it was difficult for me to comprehend. I was simply going to buy some sodas—the opposite of anything hostile.

For what felt more like an eternity than two hours, my grandfather, grandmother, mother, and uncle reminded me of these troubling realities: (1) that my dark skin, then embracing a five-feet-ten-inch, thirteen-year-old frame, was a considerable threat for some people, and (2) that some people would not be patient enough to judge me based on the content of my character but rather would be fixated on the color of my skin, and that the color of my skin, viewed through the lens of prejudice, meant that I was the physical embodiment of their greatest fear (a big Black man), a fear reinforced daily by mass media. Ever since that fateful December night, I have lived life in full knowledge of these realities.

I, a latter-generation Gen-Xer, must pass down to my postmillennial son some of the rules of engagement for a "Black man" in this society.

Having added over five inches and one hundred pounds to that thirteen-year-old frame over the years, I have learned to give quick and easy smiles when riding in elevators to disarm my fellow passengers and to assure them that they're not in imminent danger. I am mindful of my tone and the inflection of my voice when conversing in multicultural groups—as I have learned that I cannot afford to use the same terms of conversation as others. For if I slightly raise my voice, instead of describing me as *passionate* some will label me *an angry Black man*. Like countless generations of men with darker skin and different features, I have been followed while shopping in stores and stopped by police so many times without cause that I am pleasantly surprised when these everyday occurrences do not happen.

Now, I, a latter-generation Gen-Xer, must pass down to my postmillennial son some of the rules of engagement for a "Black man" in this society:

1. If the police stop you, make sure you stop in a well-lit area and don't make any sudden moves. In fact, verbally broadcast your actions (to illustrate, "Officer, I am now reaching into the glove compartment for my registration").
2. Always get the receipt after making a purchase, no matter how inexpensive, so no one can accuse you falsely of theft later.
3. It doesn't matter if the other kids are "doing it," whatever *it* is. Your punishment will always be much more severe if you are caught doing the same. This is also true in adulthood.

I must inform my son that on account of the color of his skin—even if he graduates with high honors from an Ivy League law school, serves as the editor of that prestigious school's law review, and goes on to be elected the president of the United States of America—some people will consider him unqualified for the job and question whether he is a "true" American. I will tell him about James Byrd Jr., the fake drug scandal of Dallas, the Tulia drug busts, and other contemporary instances of societal racism in our home state of Texas, even as previous generations of Black fathers have spoken to their sons of Emmett Till, the Tuskegee Experiment, and COINTELPRO.

And, yes, I will tell him about Troy Anthony Davis. I will tell my son that even in the face of compelling doubt surrounding conviction and the cries of other nations to spare his life, joined with the pleas of former US presidents and Nobel laureates, poison could likewise be injected into his veins. For, in the eyes of some, my son is considered to be an animal that must be put down at all costs.

I will take part in this familiar yet painful ritual, for as the apostle Paul articulated to his sons and daughters in the faith, I would not want my son "to be unaware . . . of the affliction we experienced" (2 Cor. 1:8).

Then I will tell my son, "Go and change the world!"

CHECK TWO

"Who is that?" my son inquired, pointing to an image on the computer screen.

"That is George Zimmerman," I replied.

"What did he do?"

"He hurt someone really badly, and the person died."

"Why?"

One of life's hardest tasks comes in answering a young child's questions about the presence of evil and tragedy in the world. I found myself challenged to tell my son that sometimes people hurt other people because they do not like them and because of the color of their skin. So, I told my son about Trayvon Martin, about how he was killed, and about what was now being done to bring justice for his death. I asked my son if he understood what I was trying to tell him. He said, "Yes," then returned to playing. He did not understand. But I knew that one day he must, and it will be my responsibility as his father to ensure that he does.

CYPHER

Dear God,
Forgive us for our failures to value life.
In Jesus' name. Amen.

 **KEEP THE FLOW**

Have you ever experienced prejudice on account of appearance? If so, how did you respond? Have you ever had to address your own prejudices against others? How has your family prepared you to face life, including its injustice?

PART THREE

JUSTICE

JUSTICE

Anyone who knows me, even marginally, recognizes that I have been greatly inspired by the legacy, ministry, and writings of Dr. Martin Luther King Jr. His life is a study in servant leadership, selflessness, commitment to the pursuit of justice, and much more. One of my favorite texts is his first book, *Stride toward Freedom: The Montgomery Story*. This book contains innumerable enlightening quotations. I was blessed to find and purchase a picture of King that contains my favorite quote from the book: "True peace is not merely the absence of tension, it is the presence of justice."

God has called us to be peacemakers, but peace without justice is no peace at all. God has also called us to be pursuers of justice. As posed hypothetically by the prophet Micah, "[God] has told you, O mortal, what is good; and what does the Lord require of you but to do justice, and to love kindness, and to walk humbly with your God?" (Mic. 6:8). The fight for justice can often be an arduous one, but it is always a necessary one.

As a seminarian, I began a civil rights pilgrimage at the university. The pilgrimage took students over spring break to cities and sites significant to the civil rights movement, to speak with the workers in the movement about their experiences and their continued hopes for justice. My interests in creating the pilgrimage were far greater than sponsoring an extended field trip for class credit. I deeply hoped that walking in the hallowed footsteps of people from previous generations who committed and sacrificed their lives in the name of justice, a new generation of "foot soldiers" would be inspired to commit themselves to the ongoing struggle for freedom and equality.

Many injustices remain in our society and across the world. Admittedly, these wrongs can easily overwhelm someone trying to decide which ones to confront. Many of the original civil rights workers we encountered on our pilgrimages suggested that today's issues are far more complex and difficult to address than those in their day. Yet, this does not mean we ignore the injustices of the day. Each generation is gifted with the sacred opportunity to complete what previous generations had started.

Our commitment should remain until the words of the pledge of allegiance fully ring true: "with liberty and justice for all."[1]

THE LITURGY
OF TRAYVON MARTIN
SKITTLES, ICED TEA, AND A HOODIE

CHECK ONE

Like many Americans, I was deeply troubled by the senseless death of seventeen-year-old Trayvon Martin, who was killed by George Zimmerman on February 26, 2012, in Sanford, Florida. The unarmed teenager was shot to death as he was returning to his father's home in a gated community after purchasing a few items from the store. Primary in his possession on that fateful night were a cell phone, rather standard fare for most Americans today, and two items from the store: a bag of Skittles candy and a can of iced tea. On that rainy evening, Trayvon also donned a hooded sweatshirt, most commonly referred to today as a hoodie.

The fact that an unarmed Black teenager in America in 2012 would be killed for looking "suspicious" is disturbing, to say the least. But the fact that his adult attacker, who himself possessed a criminal record, walked as a free man for many weeks before charges were filed against him—charges more likely the result of the public's outcry than the administration of justice—was more than disturbing. It was tragic!

Across the nation, as marches and rallies organized to seek justice for Trayvon Martin, several symbols emerged as part of the call to justice: the hoodie, bags of Skittles, and canned iced tea. As I witnessed it, this phenomenon inspired me to assign meaning to these symbols, not just to encourage myself in the wake of this tragedy but also to provide myself and others the opportunity to consider our role in ensuring that a tragedy like this does not happen again.

Symbols have long been important for religious and spiritual reflection. Symbols have been employed to provide greater understanding of transcendent truths, to provide comfort amid chaos, and to inspire faithful action for the common good. Many times symbols have emerged from rather mundane objects closely associated with a historical event.

Before his passion, Christ blessed and broke bread as a symbol of his body, soon to be battered and bruised. He blessed and poured wine as a symbol of his blood, which was soon to pour from his open wounds. These rather ordinary objects, bread and wine, are symbols that remain central to Christian worship today when celebrating the Eucharist.

And that wooden Roman instrument of public execution, the cross, has emerged as the primary symbol of the Christian faith. I have always wondered how baffling and unnerving it would be for a first-century Roman citizen to see a known instrument of death now adorned with gold and jewels, draping countless necks, and displayed in houses of worship and homes across the world. The cross as a symbol now transcends Roman execution and is widely held as a symbol of victory.

Consider the murder of seventeen-year-old Trayvon Martin. Three rather mundane objects have emerged as greater symbols of reflection. These objects help us to reflect on the historic and ongoing persecution of Black masculinity in America and a newly energized movement to end that persecution: Skittles, iced tea, and the hoodie. It has been reported widely that as he was being followed that fateful night, Trayvon covered his head with his hoodie, to conceal himself from his pursuer. Unarmed, his possessions were a single bag of Skittles and a can of iced tea.

What do Skittles, iced tea, and the hoodie now symbolize? What greater meaning do they possess?

Since Trayvon's death, thousands have marched in protest, themselves donning hoodies; and thousands more have posted, shared, and tweeted photos of the same throughout social media. Bags of Skittles have been mailed by protesters to authorities and have been creatively incorporated into signs of protest. Iced tea has remained central in our discourse and dialogue on the tragedy. But what do Skittles, iced tea, and the hoodie now symbolize? What greater meaning do they possess? How can these objects form a new liturgy, not only for reflecting on the life and death of Trayvon Martin but for all who seek "to do justice, and to love kindness, and to walk humbly with your God" (Mic. 6:8)? I humbly propose the following:

Skittles possess a hard, sugary shell in a multiplicity of flavors and colors, held together in a single package. The liturgy of Trayvon Martin inspires us to rid our nation of systemic racism and consider that although, like Skittles, we Americans come in a multiplicity of "flavors" (read preferences) and colors, we are still held together in unity in the single packaging of being created in the image of God. It is forever true that each of us has been endowed by the Creator with the right to life, liberty, and the pursuit of happiness.

Sweetened iced tea, a staple of Southern culture, refreshes the parched palate. Tea, however, does not originally emerge in sweetened form. Its sweetness is the result of an intentional action to remove its bitterness. The liturgy of Trayvon Martin reminds us that in our quest for justice against all forms of injustice and prejudice we must remain sweet, not bitter, lest we become what we oppose. This will take intentionality on our part, for it is easy to confuse revenge with justice. We do no justice to Trayvon's memory by likewise embodying the bitter racism that took his life.

The liturgy of Trayvon Martin reminds us that the season of our fight against injustice may turn bitterly cold, but we must remain resolute and hooded in our commitment.

The hoodie, that hooded sweatshirt of particular popularity within urban America, was first designed by Champion in the 1930s to provide warmth to workers who had to endure freezing temperatures. The liturgy of Trayvon Martin reminds us that the season of our fight against injustice may turn bitterly cold, but we must remain resolute and hooded in our commitment that we "not grow weary in doing what is right" (Gal. 6:9) and endure to the end.

Let Skittles, iced tea, and the hoodie become symbols of truth, inspiration, and comfort for a new generation of protesters against the ongoing crucifixion of innocent flesh at the hands of a corrupt system of oppression and marginalization that has for too long tortured the masses and tainted our country's legacy.

Amen.

CHECK TWO

Fifty years ago, three caskets containing the mutilated bodies of three young girls rested before Dr. Martin Luther King Jr. as he spoke from the pulpit of Sixteenth Street Baptist Church in Birmingham.

A month prior, King spoke, "I have a dream that my four little children will one day live in a nation where they will not be judged by the color of their skin but by the content of their character." King's hopes for his own children would not be realized in the girls eulogized. In "Eulogy for the Martyred Children," King stated, "They have something to say to each of us in their death. . . . They say to us that we must be concerned not merely about who murdered them, but about the system, the way of life, the philosophy, which produced the murderers."

King's words ring true as we mourn anew the murder of Trayvon Martin and the acquittal of his killer, George Zimmerman. While Zimmerman was the killer, the greatest threat to Trayvon Martin, and to young Black boys across this nation, is the "system" and its prevailing philosophies. The system's philosophies, rooted in our nation's dark history of racism, unjustly categorized Trayvon Martin as both criminal and dangerous, and were used as justification of Zimmerman's deadly interests.

This system has tried, convicted, and executed many Black boys without cause, both inside our nation's courts and on our nation's streets. Black boys walking in gated communities and listening to music in their vehicles, as evidenced by the murder of Jordan Davis, have been treated as if their mundane actions warranted deadly force. Young Black boys have been tried, convicted, and executed by a system that finds their Black masculinity an offense, rendering them guilty until proven innocent.

Four little girls were not the only children to die on that fateful Sunday in 1963. Also murdered that day in Birmingham was a young Black boy named Virgil Ware, thirteen, shot in the face and chest while riding on the handlebars of his brother's bicycle, an action warranted, by someone, as a capital offense.

King closed the eulogy with a nod to Shakespeare: "And today, as I stand over the remains of these beautiful, darling girls, I paraphrase . . . 'Good night, sweet princesses. Good night, those who symbolize a new day. And may the flight of angels take thee to thy eternal rest.'"

While I bid sweet rest to our beautiful princes Emmett Till, Virgil, Trayvon, Jordan, and countless others, and peace to their families, it is this cruel and corrupt system that I hope soon will be put to rest.

CYPHER

Dear God,
Liturgies require movement. Liturgies require contemplation
and committed action informed by that contemplation. Help us to
commit our thoughts and our actions to the cause of justice
and to remain fortified in that commitment until the words
of the prophet are fulfilled: "Let justice roll down like waters,
and righteousness like an ever-flowing stream."
In Jesus' name. Amen.

 **KEEP THE FLOW**

What other new symbols can be appropriated by your community to inspire new movements? What can your community do to oppose unjust systems?

SEEKING SHAQUAN
A CALL FOR INCREASED MALE PRESENCE IN PUBLIC EDUCATION

CHECK ONE

Emblazoned across the stomach of the late Tupac Shakur was arguably one of the most famous tattoos in the history of popular culture. "T.H.U.G. L.I.F.E." became a midnineties mantra that echoed from the inner city to suburbia to the wide open spaces of rural America.

Tupac was a complex and controversial artist, and the message intended by his tattoo was often assumed to convey something sinister or criminal in nature. In fact, the opposite is true. Tupac's tattoo served as a heartbreaking—yet honest and even prophetic—word for a nation sorely neglecting the youngest members of its society. The acronym stood for: "The hate you give little infants f***** everyone."

While you might disagree with Tupac's choice of words, no one can disagree with the validity of this statement. When children suffer from neglect, it not only impacts them but also has long-standing and immeasurable ramifications for our community as a whole. Considering the social, political, economic, and spiritual landscapes of America today, it appears as though our youth are largely being left behind. This is especially true of young African American men.

Today only 47 percent of African American men graduate from high school; at the same time, funding for youth programs and music and arts programs in schools is being eliminated. Furthermore, many of the family systems from which these young men emerge continue to be in disarray. The sad result of our failures as adults has been the creation of a generation of young people who carry little esteem for themselves, little respect for others, and who harbor bitter pain at the core of their being.

Because of my great concern for the future of our nation and the future of our young people, I spend considerable time engaging our public schools. A recent visit to a school yielded for me yet another disturbing reality: the lack of men present to teach young men in our educational system.

F ew artistic expressions possess as much personal meaning for me as *The Miseducation of Lauryn Hill*. Anytime I listen, that music transports me back to my college years, to the blossoming of new love (when dating my wife, our first song was "Nothing Even Matters," a duet by Lauryn and D'Angelo, featured on the album), back to the final moments of the last century that feel like simpler times, oddly enough.

In addition to the songs on the album, equally captivating are the interludes, wherein a male "teacher," played by hip-hop activist and current Newark City councilman Ras J. Baraka, leads his young "students" in an engaging dialogue on the meaning of love. The first interlude serves as a roll call of students. When Lauryn's name is called, there is no response, highlighting her presumed absence from class.

From the first time I listened to this interlude, and every time since, another name, not Lauryn's, has reigned prominently over the others. It is that of ShaQuan Sutton. The name stands out for no other reason than its auditory appeal. Recently, however, I have begun to envision the endless promise for ShaQuan's life, given the context of his factious educational upbringing. For ShaQuan and his "classmates" experienced something that escaped much of my own educational experience, as well as the educational experiences of countless youth today—a strong, nurturing male presence in the classroom.

I recently served as Principal for a Day at a local elementary school. I invited members of my congregation to join me that day as we coordinated our continued efforts to support public education. Upon arriving on campus, I was greeted by a cadre of extraordinary professional women: the administrative office manager, the guidance counselor, the assistant principal, the principal. I would meet dozens more accomplished women throughout the day. Yet, as the day progressed, my maleness loomed large.

When I inquired as to how our church could best assist the school, I was told, "We need men!"

The principal informed me that in her school of five hundred students and sixty staff persons, only two men were part of the professional staff. One was a coach. Only one man taught in the classroom setting. When two men from my congregation arrived, our collective presence doubled the average adult male presence on the campus!

The impact of our presence was immediate and discernible. Teachers noted that as I read the morning announcements, students quieted, sat up straight, and listened intently. I spoke at an assembly on the topic of bullying and informed any bullies that they would that day be meeting with me in the office. No such student reported to the office that day. Many mentioned that the campus "felt" different with the presence of men.

When I inquired as to how our church could best assist the school, I was told, "We need men! Men to serve as mentors. Men to read to our students. Men to sit and have lunch with our students. Men who will be present in the lives of our students."

This experience caused me to pause and to reflect on my own educational journey. I had reached the sixth grade before I had male teachers in the classroom. I was a senior in college before I took a course taught by a Black man. I came to recognize that the absence of men in my educational experience, especially men of color, propelled me, in my first time as a graduate student, to take every course I could that was being taught by an African American male scholar. And it's likely the reason why my doctoral committee was headed by a Puerto Rican man, an African American woman, and an African American man. I was making up for lost time, seeking now what was lacking then—a nurturing and empowering male presence in my educational experience.

I, like many, had previously noted the impact of male absenteeism in society, especially in the family. But I had failed to see the impact of male absence on our youth in the educational process. Is it possible that declining interest in the pursuit of education among men is their understanding of its being a primarily female pursuit?

I fully recognize that there are men, including men of color, who, as teachers, coaches, administrators, and volunteers, actively nurture and empower our youth. I honor them for their commitment and effort! However, our educational process is producing too few ShaQuan Suttons—young people whose educational journeys have been positively shaped and empowered by male teachers.

So I ponder several questions: What positive impact does male presence have upon the educational experience of today's ShaQuan Suttons? What can ShaQuan Suttons grow to become with their lives shaped early on by a nurturing male presence in the classroom?

My maternal grandfather died at the age of eighty-three. For forty-four of those years, he worked in public education as a biology teacher, a coach, a bus driver, a principal, and, before retirement, as an assistant superintendent. At his funeral and for months following his death, men from across the nation came to offer their respects. Many claimed that the time they spent with my grandfather changed their lives and that the lessons he taught them not only shaped them intellectually but gave them greater vision of what it means to be a man. Grown men, many now seniors themselves, testified with tears in their eyes to the impact this male educator had on their lives!

We desperately need more male involvement in public education so that in the future, when the roll is called for a new generation of young people who will be productive citizens, those students can answer the roll as ShaQuan Sutton did: "Here!"

CHECK TWO

In recent days, I have grown gravely concerned not only with the lack of a productive presence of men within our homes, churches, and schools but also with articles and reports now claiming—directly or indirectly—that the role of men is inconsequential, especially in the African American community. While I acknowledge that, generally speaking, African American men have been woefully absent, I must also acknowledge that their absence has resulted in far more bad than anyone could ever attempt to imagine as good.

Statistically speaking, when men are absent, families are poorer; children are more endangered and likely to fall into depression, violence, and addiction. It is, therefore, imperative that all men of goodwill take the extra step of expressing care and concern not only for the young men who are in their direct garden of influence but for other young men who lack the care and compassion of a concerned and present male.

One day at a public school changed the atmosphere of the entire campus. How much more could men change the atmosphere of our society with their presence and with a commitment to seek out "ShaQuans" wherever they can be found in order to mentor them?

CYPHER

Dear God,
Raise up a generation of men who will be present, active,
and productive at home, in church, in our schools, and in our overall
communities. Give these men the strength to uplift not only their
biological sons but also the sons of men inactive or absent.
In Jesus' name. Amen.

 **KEEP THE FLOW**

What can be done to make primary and secondary education a more attractive career path for men? In what ways can more men, other than teachers, be invited to participate in the educational process? Which Black men are having a positive impact on your life or the life of your family and how?

WITH DEEPEST REGRET
A LETTER TO THE ANCESTORS

CHECK ONE

What would you write if given the opportunity to communicate with your ancestors? What would you tell them about life today? How would you express to them your gratitude for the lives they lived and for the many sacrifices they made on your behalf?

When writing to my ancestors on the 150th anniversary of the signing of the Emancipation Proclamation, I pondered long and hard as to what I would share. I had so much to say, yet felt like I had so little time and space in which to say it. The prospect of writing to my ancestors became weighty as I considered what they had endured. Images of slave ships and chains, auction blocks and whips dominated my mental cloud. So too did the screams that must have reverberated across the hills and valleys as babies were ripped from the arms of their mothers. How did my ancestors maintain their strength, their dignity, their faith in the face of such great tragedy?

When I began to write, what first formed on the page was an apology. As I have observed the present condition of too many of these former slaves' descendants, I have been deeply troubled. I see communities in peril, families in disarray, innocent life snuffed out without cause. But as I have continued to write, what has formed is more than an apology; it is a letter of condolence. I think of all the pain our present condition would have caused my ancestors, given all that they sacrificed so that we could be free. As I tried to name their pain, only one word came to mind: *bereavement*.

To the Ancestors:

With deepest regret, I must inform you of the fate that has come to your sun-kissed sons and daughters of the African diaspora, your descendants in the well over two-hundred-year-old American enterprise. Despite your audacious ambitions and prayerful petitions for the generations that succeeded you upon these shores, I must now speak to you concerning our present difficulties.

Not that our condition has not markedly improved since the days of your bonds, replete with the horrors of the auction block and the brutality of whips tearing against your flesh. Nothing within our present experience can equate to the terrors of the American slave system that you so courageously endured and fought against. Terrors the European founder of Methodism, John Wesley, called "the vilest that ever saw the sun."

You would be proud of our people's achievement since Lincoln's pen secured our emancipation *de jure* and intensified the war that secured our emancipation *de facto*. Our people have risen from chains and cotton fields to the pinnacles of industry, as well as to seats of power all over the world. Yet, despite such laudable achievements, the present struggles of many of our people remain great. The full scope of these struggles is at once horrifying and overwhelming.

Our core institutions of family, school, and church are crumbling en masse. While you endured the plight of family dissolution upon the auction block, today the great majority of our beautiful Black seeds are born outside the nurturing context of marital family commitment. Paternal absenteeism replaces the auction block and continues to rip apart generations as now many descendants continue to come of age without the knowledge or active presence of their fathers.

---

*Once deemed a vehicle of liberation,
the church appears to have lost its prophetic zeal.*

Educational pursuits, most notably the pursuit of literacy, were forbidden to you. Secretly, many of you still attained this prize, undaunted by the threat of brutal punishment or even death. The illegality of literacy has long ceased, yet our schools graduate the illiterate. And all too often it is our Black seeds that fill the ranks. Adding injury to insult, many of the schools you founded to empower future generations have closed their doors, with others perilously close to doing the same. Esteemed colleges and universities that first met in the basement of your churches and were later built into proud institutions are now in jeopardy despite hundreds of thousands, if not millions, of our seeds without a college education.

The Black church, once the epicenter of Black cultural, intellectual, and spiritual life, the forerunner in the fight for freedom and justice in America, has been relegated to an irrelevant relic in the eyes of many, perceived as disconnected from and unconcerned about the present sufferings of our people. Once deemed a vehicle of liberation, the church appears to have lost its prophetic zeal and become the "social club" of Dr. Martin Luther King Jr.'s nightmares. As a result, our communities are becoming spiritually bankrupt citadels void of revolutionary power.

Tragically, these crumbling institutions have made way for a petri dish of scourges now propagating with rapidity among our people. A deadly, incurable yet wholly preventable disease continues to ravage Black bodies. An entire nation of our beautiful, Black manhood resides behind prison walls. In countless neighborhoods, abject poverty coupled with addiction siphons out the hope of progress. Senseless violence has left many communities as war-torn wastelands.

Not that we have been unassisted in this decline. The vestiges of injustice you faced remain with us today. Daily is our fight against systems informed by systemic racism, although these systems are ofttimes veiled. Yet there is an undeniable difference between our struggles. You knew your oppressors well and directly engaged them toward the cause of liberty. Today, given the fragmentation and infighting within our own communities, present even among our most celebrated leaders, we have seemingly become enemies to one another. It appears that we have become co-conspirators in our own oppression.

Please accept my deepest sympathies on the painful loss of so many of your children, past and present.

Perhaps our greatest challenge is our fragmentation along class lines. The victories of the American civil rights movement provided opportunity and access primarily to the Black middle class. Consequently, Black flight—fleeing historic Black communities in the inner city and retreating to the suburbs—has stripped these communities of our businesses and resources, leaving behind masses of our brothers and sisters still bound by the chains of poverty. The poignant provocative that first arose from the lips of Cain, now resonates anew: "Am I my brother's keeper?" In recent years, we have appeared to respond in joint refrain, "No!"

Ultimately, I fear that in the Black community, unlike the children of Israel whose biblical narrative of emancipation secured safe passage for the entire people, we have left some behind. Some with means have broken rank, allowing the gushing waters of denied access and poverty to swallow up those of lesser means. With deepest regret, I acknowledge our failure to advance fully the cause of freedom and justice you first began, for after achieving comfort and privilege for the few, we seem to have forgotten the many.

It remains my sincere hope that we shall one day achieve the greatness for which you, our ancestors, fought and died. Please accept my deepest sympathies on the painful loss of so many of your children, past and present. We salute your courageous sacrifices for your people and our entire nation.

And to my oldest known ancestors, John Bell, born 1828 in Kentucky; Keizar Forbes, born 1830 in Alabama; and Reverend William Leaks, born 1835 in North Carolina, later a founder of Paul Quinn College; each born a slave:

Our family shall endeavor to make you as proud in our generation as you have made us proud in yours!

Eternally grateful, your sun-kissed son,

Michael

CHECK TWO

Several years ago, I had the opportunity to visit an old building near the banks of the Alabama River in Selma. My guide that day informed me that we were standing where many of my ancestors stood after being unloaded off the boats. They would have been held overnight, crammed into the building until auction time. The next day, they were then removed from the building, marched in chains down the road, and sold to the highest bidder. I felt both sadness and anger while standing in a place of such great atrocities against humankind.

This mixture of emotion is familiar to me. As a pastor engaged in urban ministry, I have often experienced this particular mixture while serving in a place of great atrocities against humankind. In my years of ministry, I have witnessed some terrible things!

I have witnessed a woman beaten and bloodied by an angry mob, a woman's head as it was slammed against a parked car, a woman dragged upon the ground by her hair—each woman assaulted by men. I have witnessed a man beaten by five others with guns drawn. I have witnessed young children roaming the streets at night. I have found men and women passed out in drug-and-alcohol-induced stupor.

I have also seen police show more concern for property than human life. I have seen schools utterly fail our children. I have seen grocers with outdated food still on their shelves and check-cashing stores taking advantage of "the least of these." All this and more has filled me with sadness and anger.

I have discovered that this great sadness and anger emerge from the same place, be it for my ancestors or for my people today. It emerges from a sense of knowing that none of God's children should live like this, knowing that this is far from the kingdom of God. I have deep regret for the failure of my generation to live out the true greatness for which our ancestors fought and died. I deeply regret the forces that still oppress God's people.

Nevertheless, despite all that I have witnessed, I commit, as my ancestors did, like many others do today, to keep hoping in the midst of darkness. I will continue to work with great expectation toward the breaking forth of a newer, brighter day! I still have hope that all that has been sown in tears will soon be reaped in joy (Ps. 126:5).

CYPHER

Dear God,
Give us the strength of our ancestors that we might hold
on to hope even as we encounter darkness.
In Jesus' name. Amen.

 **KEEP THE FLOW**

If you could communicate directly with your ancestors, what would you say about the world today? How are you continuing to build upon the accomplishments of those who have come before you?

TOY SOLDIERS AND AMERICA'S KILLING FIELDS

CHECK ONE

Without question we live in a violent society. Each day our news headlines are full of reports of brutal violence. We have witnessed heartbreaking images of public massacres, disturbing reports of gang shoot-outs, and troubling occurrences of police brutality. Sexual assault rages against human frames, terrorizing the human soul. Domestic abuse fiercely rages in too many homes, and road rage, well, rages on our streets. Some acts of violence occur with such frequency in particular communities that the media all but ignore these acts—with many acts, including homicides, going unreported.

Violence in America is not new. Our nation has a remarkably violent past, including slavery, genocide against Native Americans, lynch mobs, and race riots. Today there is increasing alarm at the propensity of violent acts perpetuated by and against our youth. For no one is this issue more pressing than for young

African American men. For an African American male aged six-teen to twenty-five, the number one cause of death is homicide.

And nowhere is the issue of violence, especially youth vio-lence, more pressing today than in the city of Chicago. In a recent outbreak of violence in America's third most populous city, African Americans have accounted for 76 percent of all murder victims with 86 percent of the murder victims being male. Persons aged seventeen to thirty-five have comprised the majority of these murder victims.

What is at the heart of these violent outbreaks? More often than not, it is fear. On too many street corners in too many neighborhoods all across America, it is kill or be killed.

The headlines after one Fourth of July weekend delivered unsettling news: in Chicago, seventy persons were wounded; twelve persons were killed.

In order to turn the tide of youth violence in our country, especially within the inner city, we must reach these youth with opportunity and hope. And we must work diligently to change the long-standing culture of violence in America.

J ust last year Chicago had over six hundred caskets / . . . Do you know what it feels like when people is passing?"

These are the heart-wrenching lyrics of Kanye West's "Everything I Am" from his 2007 studio album, *Graduation*. The Chicagoan's musings, now several years removed, retain relevance as Chicago continues along its seemingly unrelenting pace of homicides and other violent crimes. Although, overall, homicides are fewer this year, a recent holiday weekend in the city witnessed more bloodshed as seventy people were wounded and twelve peo-ple were killed, raising the city's homicides above two hundred. In 2012, Chicago recorded more than five hundred homicides.

Chicago's violence is attributed not just to the alarming accessibility of handguns but also to the dismantling of the hierarchy of street gangs, a result of so-called street corner conspiracy busts by police. As Tracy Siska, founder and executive director of the Chicago Justice Project noted in his paper "Gangs, Violent Crime, and the Unintended Consequences": "There is a significant increase in leaderless cliques of youths on the streets lacking any local affiliations to structure or restrain their actions. Cliques and individuals that once were affiliated now fight against each other as well as against other gangs."

In essence, young gangstas have been left to raise themselves while the O.G.s (original gangstas) are away, either serving lengthy prison sentences or dead, themselves the victims of violent crime. The dismantling of this criminal yet structurally effective leadership apparatus has resulted in "orphaned" gangstas. Without O.G.s to indoctrinate them with a street code of "ethics," these youth have increasingly created marked factions among fellow gang members now warring with one another for control of the streets.

In these young men, I find neither courage nor strength. Instead I sense reverberations of great fear; scared young men hiding behind big guns.

I love my job as an inner-city pastor, and I have witnessed God's transformative power in myself, our congregation, and the South Dallas community in which we live and serve. At times, however, my ministry context has been one of brutal violence. I have witnessed unthinkable acts of violence unleashed with unquenchable rage and malice. There was the mob of fifty people that spilled out into traffic from an apartment complex. A man who pushed a woman down and then repeatedly kicked her in the face. On witnessing this tragedy, I threw open my car door to render aid. A stunningly strong grip on the back of my clergy collar halted my exit. My wife reasoned with me and suggested that we contact the authorities instead.

She likely saved my life.

Other troubling scenes in my mind replay with a vengeance. I have witnessed terrible acts of violence unleash great bloodshed with total disregard for the sacredness of all humankind. Their faces have become blurred, but I still see these young men's eyes—eyes filled with an empty darkness emanating from deep-seated pain.

In these young men, I find neither courage nor strength. Instead I sense reverberations of great fear; scared young men hiding behind big guns. For all of their disturbing acts, these young men emerge for me as toy soldiers without a clear mission or direction, fighting in an inexplicable war for honor they do not deserve to control turf they do not own.

Yet, this war has real casualties.

Last summer, I was invited to address a Stop the Violence rally in one of Dallas's most violent zip codes. Before I offered my words, four mothers spoke. Each mother had a son who had been killed within the past year. Each murder remained unsolved. The ages of the deceased: seventeen, fifteen, fourteen, and eleven. The death of children speaks powerfully to the insanity of recent violence. This year, our national consciousness has been held captive by the murders of two Chicago youth: Hadiya Pendleton, fifteen, shot and killed in a Chicago park days after performing for President Obama's second presidential inauguration; and Jonylah Watkins, six-months-old, shot five times as her father changed her diaper.

Chicago has received national attention as a result of its alarming murder rate. Nevertheless, a proper treatment of violence cannot be limited to the inner city. Violence is not merely a Chicago problem or a South Dallas problem. It is an American problem. America's killing fields are not relegated to urban streets. We have tragically witnessed toy soldiers and America's killing fields extend from a suburban Colorado movie theater and a Wisconsin Sikh temple to an Arizona grocery store parking lot—and many places in between. Yes, the world's most industrialized nation has a violence problem, and dare I say that like toy soldiers, fear, including xenophobia, abides close to the heart of America's blood addiction.

In lyric, Kanye West also laments, "The church won't tithe, so we can't afford to stay." In years past, churches established orphanages to care for the twice bereaved. Today this important ministry continues, albeit most prominently in foreign countries. In order to save an entire generation and turn the tide of youth violence in our nation, it is incumbent on the church to renew its commitment to help raise orphans, especially these new orphans, toy soldiers engulfed by fear and hiding behind guns. The church must help to transform America's killing fields into reservoirs of hope and realized potential. It will be painstaking work; but if we in the church fail to do it, we will find the mounting cost of lost lives more than unaffordable.

It will be unbearable.

CHECK TWO

It takes substantial effort to find quality food at competitive prices in my community. South Dallas is a "food desert." There is only one true grocer that serves the entire community. It has been my frequent experience that this particular store is not well maintained, its selections grossly limited, and its produce lacking freshness.

However, my community is overrun by liquor stores with heavily hiked prices, carrying an abundance of low-quality foods. This forces many residents with limited transportation to use these liquor stores as grocers. While it is difficult to purchase groceries, it is exceedingly easy to buy liquor. Six liquor stores sit upon two short city blocks near our church alone.

South Dallas community activists report that our community has more than eighty active drug houses. I have witnessed countless drug transactions occur in clear view in broad daylight. It is easy to buy drugs in my community. It is also easy to purchase a gun from the black market in my community. You can literally walk to a street corner and return with a gun in less than two hours.

When liquor, drugs, and guns are more accessible to residents than a fresh tomato, there is an inherent sense of hopelessness. Now imagine growing up in this context. Imagine that this is the only world that you know. Now you may be able to see how such an overwhelming sense of hopelessness could hold captive the mind of a young person so that he or she feels as though there is nothing to live for.

It is imperative for the church—and people of goodwill—to reclaim a prophetic mantle and not only provide safe and empowering settings in which our young people can discover, grow, and thrive but also actively oppose the forces of evil that hold our communities captive. Quite possibly the only institutions outnumbering liquor stores in our community are churches.

What a glorious day it would be to witness the church ministering beyond its walls to manifest hope in our community anew!

CYPHER

Dear God,
Do not let our youth fall captive to hopelessness,
and help your church to oppose evil in all its forms fearlessly.
In Jesus' name. Amen.

 **KEEP THE FLOW**

What can be done to curb violent crime, especially among our youth? How can the church engage "new orphans" so that they do not turn to the streets?

PART FOUR

POP CULTURE

POP CULTURE

Throughout my life, issues of faith have been most prominent in my contemplations. My thoughts, however, have never been merely an interest in the means of personal salvation but have included an interest in people, the societies in which they live, and the role of faith in their life experiences. As such, my contemplations have often led to an engagement of popular culture, especially the intersections of religion and popular culture, the media and popular culture, and the expressions of African American religious thought in popular culture.

I have long been interested in African American cultural conceptions of God, of God's work in community, and how these conceptions have guided and supported cultural and social movements. As a seminarian, I was introduced to a mind-shaping article titled "Rap Music, Hip-Hop Culture, and 'The Future Religion of the World'" by Robin Sylvan, which made the compelling argument that hip-hop has important "implications for the larger landscape of religion in [American popular culture]."[1]

I began to question just what impact hip-hop culture has on religion and American popular culture. I began to observe more closely religious depictions in hip-hop culture. For years many rappers have worn large—often diamond-encrusted—crosses, and they have also been seen wearing pendants depicting Jesus' face. I became interested in the secularization of religious rhetoric and symbols in some parts of hip-hop culture, wherein religious rhetoric, like rapper Jay-Z's use of the alias J-Hova (which sounds like the Hebrew word for God, *Jehovah*), and religious symbols like the cross, have been disassociated from their original meanings.

Understanding that symbols and words are powerful cultural tools, I wondered what power these religious symbols and words could retain, either when assigned new, secular meanings in popular culture or when people become desensitized to their presence by overuse and possibly misguided use. My interest in popular culture has compelled me to look at popular media's depictions of African Americans, particularly African American men. In most cases, the depiction is dismal at best. This is of great concern, for these tragic images can negatively shape the young psyches of African American children, giving them little to aspire to do and be.

AN ODD FUTURE
FOR FAITH IN HIP-HOP

CHECK ONE

Hip-hop is a multicultural, multilingual, and multifaceted international movement that possesses transformational power. From its humble beginning on the streets of the South Bronx in the early 1970s as the youthful yet powerful emergent culture of largely impoverished African American and Latino youth, hip-hop culture has become a worldwide movement now extending over multiple generations. Hip-hop culture's influence has shaped and empowered communities and institutions the world over; active hip-hop movements can be found everywhere from South Africa to South America, from Paris, France, to Seoul, South Korea. Without question in my mind, hip-hop culture was the most powerful cultural movement of the last quarter of the twentieth century, and it has continued its dominance for more than a decade into the twenty-first century while showing no signs of diminishing influence any time soon.

FREESTYLE

Recent movements within the larger cultural movement of hip-hop culture have been rather disturbing. Spirituality has always been a part of hip-hop culture, especially hip-hop's primary musical artistry of rap music. While God was rarely named, reverence for the Divine often appeared in the artistry, as well as compelling inquiries related to the Divine. Yet, a certain reverence and acknowledgment of God has been on the decline recently and is seemingly replaced with aggression and opposition to God.

In recent years, sacred places, such as churches and synagogues, and sacred images, such as the cross, the Star of David, and the Torah have been desecrated in popular media. These anti-God movements are the greatest threat to hip-hop's transformational power. Given hip-hop's great international influence, these movements must be addressed or run the risk of having negative impact on future generations.

I love hip-hop! I love hip-hop music. I love hip-hop fashion. I love hip-hop culture. A multicultural, multilingual, international phenomenon, hip-hop is arguably the most significant cultural and artistic movement of the last forty years.

I am a proud member of the hip-hop generation, defined by Bakari Kitwana, former editor of *The Source* magazine, as the population of Black youth born between 1965 and 1984 (although a redefinition is likely merited to reflect hip-hop's aforementioned diversity and longevity). When I first heard the poignant inquiry of the hip-hop coming-of-age love story in the movie *Brown Sugar* (2002), "So, when did you fall in love with hip-hop?" it arrested my consciousness and caused me to reflect on the origins of my own love affair with hip-hop. (For the record, I fell in love with hip-hop when I heard A Tribe Called Quest's classic album *Midnight Marauders* (1993). It literally changed my life!)

I am also a part of an ever-widening group of young, seminary-trained clergy who closely identify with hip-hop culture: pastors, ministers, and even professors of religion for whom hip-hop was never a passing fad but an ever-present reality. It is my two-decades-old love of hip-hop that fueled my doctoral study on the contextualization of hip-hop spirituality for the church.

What others might perceive as vulgarities can actually be an authentic witness to the truth.

But at the risk of sounding out-of-touch, outdated, and even uncool—a significant risk in the realm of hip-hop—I am increasingly troubled by certain contemporary moves in hip-hop culture that embrace the occult and make a mockery of faith. I understand freedom of speech and expression. I even subscribe to the belief that what others might perceive as vulgarities can actually be an authentic witness to the truth. But I find recent attacks against religious faith and God in hip-hop to be, well, wack!

One need look no further than two hip-hop acts being heralded by many, such as *Billboard* magazine and the *New York Times*, as the future of hip-hop: rapper Lil' B and the hip-hop collective Odd Future Wolf Gang Kill Them All. Lil' B is also known by his rap alias, "Based God," and the cover of his mixtape *Angels Exodus* depicts the artist crucified on a cross, wearing a crown of marijuana, with money spilling from his shirt pockets and a bra and G-string draped across the horizontal beam. In one of his more controversial songs "Look Like Jesus," Lil' B raps that he receives fellatio due to his resemblance to Jesus Christ. In the accompanying video, he performs these lyrics while in a church sanctuary.

Many of Odd Future's lyrics promote the rape of women and make light of school massacres. Their mantra "Kill People, Burn S***, F*** School" has been known to whip concertgoers into frenzied fits of violence. They also feature anti-Christ and anti-Christian lyrics. In their popular song "Sand-witches," Hodgy Beats of Odd Future raps that "God is the cancer."

Now the hip-hop of my youth was far from Sunday school material. Some of it was replete with misogyny, violence, and rampant drug use. Yet, despite these vices, there was still a certain reverence for the Divine. While there has long been a subgenre in hip-hop music known as Horrorcore, with its "horror-themed lyrical content and imagery," never before has Horrorcore been so readily accepted and embraced by the mainstream. Even the most gangsta of rappers inevitably tipped their hat to God. In the classic song "It Was a Good Day" from his album *The Predator* (1992), Ice Cube gives reverence to the Divine with the lyric, "Just waking up in the morning gotta thank God" prior to departing for his drunken, gun-toting, promiscuity-laden day.

I won't deny the tremendous talent of Lil' B or Odd Future. However, I find their lyrics and imagery to be destructive, sacrilegious, blasphemous, and ultimately dangerous to the social, physical, intellectual, and spiritual well-being of their most impressionable listeners.

A closer listen to their music also reveals another disturbing element of our contemporary experience, one for which they are not at fault: paternal absenteeism and its impact on emerging generations. In his song "Bastard," Tyler the Creator of Odd Future predictably rails against God. But his rhymes also reveal a serious void left by the absence of his father with lyrics such as "f*** a deal," I just want my father's e-mail, so I can tell him how much I f****** hate him in detail."

Could it be that, because the church has failed to reach them and fathers have largely abandoned them, we have produced a generation now coming of age who express their angst and pain in ways that are destructive to themselves, their spirituality, and their communities?

We have been awakened to odd days in hip-hop.

And if such blasphemous content continues, hip-hop will have an odd future indeed!

CHECK TWO

Thankfully, newly released and acclaimed albums have reintroduced faith contemplation into mainstream hip-hop. Among the most heralded of these offerings are Kendrick Lamar's *good kid, m.A.A.d. city,* Kanye West's *Yeezus,* and Jay-Z's *Magna Carta Holy Grail.* In West's new song "I Am a God," he raps about being a god and a man of God, acknowledging that his life is held in God's hands. What Kanye has done is substantial from a Christian point of view, in that he's managed to push religious discussion into mainstream pop culture.

I believe that hip-hop culture offers great promise for the future of faith and the church, and many people are awakening to this reality. For entire generations of unchurched persons, especially those shaped by an urban contemporary context, the sacred utterances of hip-hop artists are canonical. Many opportunities have surfaced for engaging hip-hop culture to reach these unchurched generations with the gospel of Jesus Christ.

Hip-hop culture allows for the creation of intergenerational dialogue within the church; the encouragement of authentic engagement with challenging subject matter within the church such as suicide, violence, addiction, poverty, and human suffering; and the affirmation of authentic struggle with deep and meaningful theological inquiries such as theodicy, temptation, and God's judgment. Hip-hop is a transcendent art form and culture wherein culture, ethnicity, class, language, and religion do not hinder the transmission of the culture. This often gives people a sense of belonging, and they feel welcomed just as they are. Being true to self or "keeping it real" remains a hallowed truth among the culture's adherents.

This sense of belonging has created a diversity in the hip-hop community that offers hope for the future of the world community and the church. Hip-hop's transcendent communication reveals that the human family shares in the search for spirituality and creates a community for engagement around that searching.

The future of faith in hip-hop now appears hopeful and the opportunities toward strengthening the church abundant!

CYPHER

Dear God,
Help us celebrate the creativity given us to
benefit others and never to create negativity.
In Jesus' name. Amen.

 **KEEP THE FLOW**

What role does spirituality play in your life? What nonreligious texts or art forms have strengthened your faith in God or ministered to you in your time of need?

STAY SCHEMIN'
THE MEDIA'S CURIOUS PORTRAYAL
OF BLACK ACHIEVEMENT

CHECK ONE

I hate to see the achievements of young people devalued!

Young people possess tremendous gifts, and in those gifts we can readily find strength and inspiration for the whole of our society. It is no mistake that many major human movements toward the empowerment of all peoples have originated from the vision and action of young people. From Martin Luther King Jr. to Nelson Mandela, Diane Nash to Angela Davis, all of them were relatively young when they took upon themselves the mantle of justice. There is a certain fearlessness, a certain courage that allowed the young people of our past to march amid dogs and fire hoses, sit in at lunch counters, and travel on integrated buses into the heart of a dangerous, segregated South. And there remains a certain strength and courage that has allowed young, marginalized inner-city dwellers to create hip-hop as a cultural movement that has now taken over the world, to mobilize against corporate greed, and to march against violence and discrimination today.

Any time a young person succeeds in life, that success is a cause for celebration, especially when consideration is given to all the threats, difficulties, and obstacles that many young people face today. That is why I found the negative reports being showered upon Justin Combs, the son of hip-hop mogul Sean "P. Diddy" Combs, so disturbing. Justin had earned and accepted a full athletic scholarship to UCLA. Here was a young man who had earned a scholarship to play college football but was being castigated by the media, crucified for his success, and treated as though he were in error for accepting that which he had worked so hard to achieve.

And since I hate to see young people devalued, I wrote the following to defend Justin against what I perceived as the media's curious portrayal of Black achievement, mainly his and that of his relatively young father.

Two years ago, in celebration of his son Justin Dior Combs's sixteenth birthday, Sean "P. Diddy" Combs purchased him a $360,000 silver Maybach. The media promptly attacked Mr. Combs for his benevolence toward his child. Mr. Combs was accused of setting a poor example for Justin by giving him such an extravagant gift at such a young age.

Furthermore, the media offered a grim outlook of Justin's future based on that gift: *Justin would never know the benefit of hard work. Justin would be irreparably spoiled rotten. Justin would be content just to live off his father's name and money.*

They were wrong. Dead wrong! (Biggie Smalls reference intended.)

Instead of becoming the spoiled, lazy, uninspired young man of the media's misguided dreams, Justin has emerged as a young man with his head on straight. He graduated with a 3.75 GPA from a prestigious private school.

He also showed athletic prowess and undoubtedly committed hundreds of hours to studying film, to weight training and off-season workouts to maximize his natural gifts. And as a result of his tremendous effort, both in the classroom and on the playing field, the University of California at Los Angeles offered Justin a full scholarship to play football for the Bruins.

Bravo, young man!

With Justin, the media had the opportunity to celebrate a notable achievement. Unlike 50 percent of young people in many parts of this country who drop out of high school each year, Justin Combs stayed the course. Unlike thousands of young people who never progress in their education beyond high school, Justin Combs has. Unlike thousands of youth from well-heeled families who are of the spoiled, lazy, and uninspired variety, Justin Combs has steered clear of trouble, a tremendous achievement given the fact that he has come of age under a microscope.

Instead of celebrating Justin's achievements, the media has found cause and opportunity to attack his family all over again: *What a poor example Mr. Combs is now setting for Justin! With his wealth, Mr. Combs should just pay for his son's tuition out of pocket. How dare Mr. Combs allow his son to take money that could be used to send some poor, struggling kid to college.*

UCLA responded. Justin's scholarship will not keep some poor, struggling kid from receiving an education. The money for Justin's scholarship, as well as over two hundred other scholarships awarded to student-athletes by UCLA this year, comes from a fund altogether separate: one set aside specifically for student-athletes, a fund supported in large part by athletic department receipts. Case closed, right?

You're wrong. You're dead wrong!

The attacks continued: *The ethical thing for Mr. Combs to do is to give a gift to the school's general fund if Justin accepts the scholarship. Anything less than one million dollars would be an insult given Mr. Combs's wealth.*

The unmitigated gall of the media (and admittedly, many within the public realm) to question the integrity of Justin Combs's acceptance of this earned scholarship. Is Justin the first child of privilege to be offered and to accept a scholarship? Hardly! Will he be the last? Absolutely not!

In Justin Combs we find a young man who has studied, competed, worked hard, and been fairly rewarded for his efforts. He could have adopted the mind-set of many heirs of wealth: sit back, enjoy your life of privilege, and wait until you can fully cash in on your inheritance. Instead, he became the young man of whom any parent would justifiably be proud.

What a curious portrayal of Justin's achievements by the media!

What a curious portrayal of Justin's achievements by the media! Since when did being rich exclude you from receiving perks? Receiving perks is one of the main perks of being rich. Rich people are often beneficiaries at others' expense. Corporate CEO bonuses and tax breaks for the wealthy are but two examples of the perks of the wealthy. Justin Combs did not receive his scholarship because he was rich. He earned it. Yet the media has portrayed him and his father in the same light as Wall Street CEOs who accept major bonuses while simultaneously laying off thousands.

Something far more sinister is at work here. Mr. Combs earned his wealth making people dance, making them look good, and through wise marketing and investments. Diddy has been wildly successful, and, as such, he is being made to pay the price for his successes. This is often the case when it comes to the media's portrayal of Black achievement. Often an asterisk is assigned to the achievement to diminish it, even with no evidence of impropriety.

Let's be clear. This is not about Justin Combs. This is not about UCLA. This is about Diddy! And this is about the media's often curious portrayal of Black achievement, a portrayal that finds no inconsistency in attacking you on account of your wealth for purchasing your son a car he did not earn *and* for not taking from him a scholarship that he did earn.

No one has the right to deny this young man the rewards of his achievement or this father his pride in that achievement. And since none of us was with Diddy while he was "shootin' in the gym" (read "working hard and earning profits"), we have no right to tell him how to spend his money. If you do . . .

You're dead wrong!

CHECK TWO

Far too often, hostilities against young people appear as the order of the day. Sadly, adult society can present clear and present dangers to the future of our young people. I consider the underfunding of educational programs and cuts to other essential programming for young people a direct assault on them. Add to these cuts the criminalization of youth culture—where youth are treated with an air of suspicion while adult criminals responsible for the collapse of entire economic frameworks and the destruction of entire ecosystems go on with nothing more than a slap on their wrists.

As sad a statement as it is to make, in many ways elder generations have let newer generations down. Elder generations have often been selfishly absent from the home and so consumed in their own lives that they have failed to impart necessary support, wisdom, and direction to the generations following them. I pray that our society will once again see young people for what they are—our most precious resource. Without the presence and uplifting of young people, there is no hope for a more faithful and glorious future through them for the benefit of us all.

Justin Combs gains national attention due to his father's celebrity. Yet countless other young people's achievements go unnoticed and are, at worst, devalued.

<u>CYPHER</u>

Dear God,
We thank you for the lives of young people.
Thank you for the transformational gifts they possess. Thank you for
the confidence and courage with which they live. Help us never to
tear young people down, regardless of their successes or failures; help us to
seek out ways to encourage, support, and lift them up always.
In Jesus' name. Amen.

 **<u>KEEP THE FLOW</u>**

What power do communities possess in addressing the media's negative depictions of them? How are the achievements of young people celebrated in your faith community?

A DIFFERENT WORLD
THE POSTMILLENNIAL PERILS OF BLACK FAMILY TV PROGRAMMING

CHECK ONE

Parenthood has a way of changing your outlook on and sensitivity to what once were seemingly common media expressions to you. As a parent, you become acutely aware of the fact that you are primarily responsible for your child's growth and development. And, you also become acutely aware of the overabundance of threats that would stunt your child's growth and development. Thus, as a parent, you morph into an arch defender for your child against such threats.

The most commonly considered threats to a child's growth and development and, thus, his or her future, are illegal drugs and alcohol, sexual activity, and violence. However, media consumption also deserves parental attention as a credible threat to the growth and development of future generations. Media depictions of drugs and alcohol, sexual activity, and violence, often without consequence, are as grave a threat to the child as the illicit ills themselves; these depictions have an impact on a child's mind and soul, providing a false reality.

A consideration of the legacy of *race* makes certain media depictions an even more credible threat for some than others. The media has had a dubious reputation at times when it comes to the depiction of minorities. Historically, there has been little balance, with most minorities being depicted in stereotypical fashion and leaning toward pathological frameworks. Within my lifetime, I can recall only one period of time during my childhood when images of promising and successful Blacks were readily accessible to viewers. And when considering that time juxtaposed to the present, today's TV programming still leaves me wanting.

An incredible evening of viewing television programming with our children inspired the following piece. Our children were completely captivated by one of their parents' favorite shows of all time *The Cosby Show*. Seeing that the episode held our children completely enthralled, I began to reflect on how Black television programming had changed over the years since my childhood, and I began to consider sorrowfully the state of television programming that my children stand to inherit.

Growing up in the mid-eighties, my friends and I practically *lived* outside! We played football—I most commonly with the distinction of being "all-time quarterback" while guiding both teams on historic drives up and down our street. We raced our bikes downhill only to ascend the hill to race down all over again. We shared in games of basketball in my friend Rahim's backyard, then chased after Pam, the prettiest girl on the block, who conveniently lived across the street from Rahim, expressing our undying love and devotion to her. When in need of nourishment, we spent much of our allowance at the candy house. And after devouring our treats, we resumed play.

Only two forces exerted enough power to stop us midplay and send us sprinting to our houses. One was the streetlights coming on and the subsequent fear of discipline for not being indoors.

The other, the top of NBC's Thursday night lineup! For an entire hour, our young eyes remained glued to our television screens. The characters we watched were articulate, beautiful, educated, engaging, humorous, and inspiring. These characters also looked like us. My early conceptions of family, fatherhood, higher education, and professional life were shaped by both *The Cosby Show* and *A Different World*. For much of my childhood, the Friday morning bus ride to school was spent recounting with my friends favorite scenes from the night before.

The Cosby Show and A Different World *were not only entertaining but relevant—tackling important social issues in a groundbreaking fashion.*

One recent evening, our young family had a free night to sit down and watch an hour of television programming together, an admitted rarity. We began to peruse the prime-time lineup for an empowering, inspiring, uplifting family show. Equipped with far more channels than the basic channels of the majority of my childhood years, we clicked our remote in search of well-acted, well-scripted entertainment for families, similar to the ones of my youth.

What we encountered were all but.

Images of women purporting to be housewives and fighting in public places.

Click.

A sitcom whose story line revolved around the frequency of the characters' sexual conquests with each other.

Click.

A singing and dancing competition.

Click.

Yet another singing and dancing competition.

Click.

Our saving grace that evening? A *Phineas and Ferb* marathon.

To be clear, African Americans are not a monolithic people. Such cannot be attributed to any ethnic group. But based on many of the most prominent depictions of Black life on television today, which are few and far between, it would appear that when depicting Black people, pathology is the order of the day. I am not suggesting that every Black character on television be a doctor or lawyer with five children, and I am not suggesting that all programming be created for family viewing. Yet rarely today are we afforded a depiction of smart, intelligent, inspiring Black characters that can be enjoyed within a family and who give us something to celebrate rather than to frown about.

The Cosby Show and *A Different World* were not only entertaining but relevant—tackling important social issues in a groundbreaking fashion when other shows dared not touch them. Racism, teenage pregnancy, HIV/AIDS, the impact of divorce on children, and many other issues were engaged to bring clarity and greater insight to these issues as well as to encourage dialogue around them. And *A Different World* is credited with swelling the enrollment of Historically Black Colleges and Universities (HBCUs), a noteworthy and unparalleled achievement for television in any era.

Last week, after a day full of activity, our family returned home to occupy our living room. As our children began to play enthusiastically with their toys on the floor in front of us, a rerun of *The Cosby Show* came on. My wife and I watched as Vanessa and her short-lived singing group, The Lipsticks, received much-needed voice lessons and were later torn asunder by Clair Huxtable for their too-revealing attire and dance moves.

I briefly paused from our viewing to behold the radiance of my wife's smile and glassy, happy eyes that had been made moist by the intensity of her laughter. Then I gazed at our children. They had ceased their play—an unusual occurrence—and were watching *The Cosby Show* intently, seemingly entranced by what was before them.

I was amazed! Almost thirty years later, the show still has the power to stop children midplay!

As the episode concluded, my son asked, "Can we watch another one?" His echo, our daughter, quickly followed behind with a shortened inquiry, "Another one?" And while I was all too happy to oblige, I was deeply concerned as well. For it appears that to find meaningful Black family television programming in the new millennium, we must return to the old one.

It's a different world from where we came from.

CHECK TWO

"Oh, no!"

"What's wrong?" I asked my wife.

"They are showing that commercial again!"

A certain maker of women's lingerie had cleverly marketed their apparel during a recent Christmas season by incorporating traditional Christmas music into their commercials. As the music played, images of scantily clad women in various states of contortion came across our screen. And according to my wife, each time the commercial played, our barely school-age son would come racing from his room.

In his school music class, my son had been learning many of the traditional Christmas songs. With childlike innocence, when the commercial first played, he came racing into the living room because he heard a song that he had recently learned, knew well, and liked. My wife and I were not so sure anymore if the music was still his only inspiration for racing into the living room.

Click.

Not only have we had to be wary of television programming and commercials, but we must now vet cartoons, even the ones played on children's channels.

One of the positive effects of the propensity of such negative programming is that it forces us more often than not to turn off the television altogether and engage one another more directly. And as long as *The Cosby Show* and *A Different World* are accessible by DVD, our family will be gifted with strong and positive Black family programming for years to come.

CYPHER

Dear God,
As parents, we desire to protect our children from all possible threats.
Yet this proves impossible as we cannot be with our children
every waking moment for the rest of their lives.
But, God, you are able to provide constant watch over them.
So we pray that you will bless us as parents
to shield our children from the threats that we can see
and to trust you to shield our children
from the threats that escape our sight.
In Jesus' name. Amen.

 **KEEP THE FLOW**

How can television and other media programming shape worldviews? What can your community do to address the negative images airing daily and having a negative impact on our youth? What entertainment can families engage in by turning off media?

KEEP FLOWING!

Let justice roll down like waters,
and righteousness like an everflowing stream.

—Amos 5:24

Terrorist attacks. Cyber attacks. Natural disasters. Mass public shootings. Domestic abuse. Corporate greed. The prison industrial complex. Racial profiling. Massive lay-offs. Home foreclosures. School closures. HIV/AIDS. Sex trafficking. Price gouging. Substance abuse. Suicide. Paternal absenteeism. Church scandals. Political scandals. Pollution. Pornography.

With all of this and more, it is easy to inquire, "Where is the hope?" The answer for these complex and sometimes disturbing times proves alarmingly simple. Hope is not gone. Hope remains where it has always been; hope lives in us.

For believers in the redemptive work of Christ, Christian hope is the "anticipation of the future as the fulfillment of God's purposes based on God's covenant faithfulness and the resurrection of Jesus Christ as known by the work of the Holy Spirit in the church."[1] We hold this confidence because we base our hope on what Christ has already accomplished. We root our hope in what God has already declared is ours!

Hope lives in all of us who are willing to keep the faith, uplift the family, speak out against injustices, stand up and fight for freedom.

Hope lives in you, hope lives in me, hope lives in all of us who are willing to keep the faith, uplift the family, speak out against injustices, stand up and fight for freedom, to give selflessly to those who are in need. Hope lives in all of us who are committed to believing in hope's redemptive qualities for our troubled world. Hope is not some flow-ery, naive emotion that is oblivious to reality. No, hope is vigilant! Hope is determined! Hope is unwavering! For hope looks at what is yet walks in the confident assurance that what should be one day will be. Hope erects new towers where old towers have fallen. And hope wakes up every morning, committed to working to bring that future and glorious reality to pass.

Hope is not immune to attack. Hope is subject to attack by fear, worry, and doubt. Yes, in times of difficulty, we may begin to question whether God's promises will actually come to pass. In times of great challenge, we may begin to wonder whether or not we will actually make it out of hard situations to experience true victory in our lives over the forces of evil within our world. Holding on to hope can be particularly challenging when what we have hoped for appears to be the furthest thing from actually happening in our time.

It is the very essence of hope that gives us the strength to endure seasons of great challenge and difficulty.

Yet in the face of these attacks, hope proves essential to life's journey. It is the very essence of hope that gives us the strength to endure seasons of great challenge and difficulty. Hope must never lose its voice!

Hope speaks to us in a strong and certain voice. Each moment of each day, hope fortifies our spirit by encouraging and reminding us that the troubles we presently experience, no matter how harrowing, will not last forever (Rom. 8:18)! Hope can make this audacious claim, for it echoes forth from the lips of God. God alone has the power to make this declaration, and thankfully God has! Our hope is rooted in God, and it is God who has spoken, "For . . . I know the plans I have for you, says the LORD, plans for your welfare and not for harm, to give you a future with hope" (Jer. 29:11).

But this is not just the future hope of glory to be revealed in the eternal presence of God. This is a hope that we can lay claim to today, a hope manifested more than two thousand years ago through the birth, ministry, public execution, and resurrection of Jesus Christ, the Son of God. It is a hope Christ himself declared as the kingdom of God; a radical new vision for all of God's creation, exemplified by love, peace, and justice.

Toward the immediacy of the kingdom of God, Christ spoke, "The kingdom of God has come to you" (Luke 11:20).

We too have the gift of the Holy Spirit to guide us into the knowledge of all truth. This truth echoes the promise of a hope-filled future in and through God. And hope emerges as the essence of our faith in God, for "faith is the assurance of things hoped for, the conviction of things not seen" (Heb. 11:1).

As children of God called to manifest hope in and to our world, we do so by walking in the promises of God, promises secured for us by the work of Christ, promises made real and true through the guidance of the Holy Spirit. And although there still remain times of great sorrow and tragedy, we face each one with the hopeful assurance that "weeping may linger for the night, but joy comes with the morning" (Ps. 30:5).

Hope tells us that the power of Jesus Christ, as manifested in and through our work, can transform all communities. Animated by the Holy Spirit, we must continue to engage the marginalized, the oppressed, the neglected communities, and the troubled culture. The freestyle hip-hop aesthetic plays a key role in hope's enterprise. Freestyle flows from the heart. As it flows, it speaks in a firm and mighty voice. In the same way, we are called to let hope flow from our hearts. When we do, we speak life.

Freestyle is most beautiful when we flow together. In the cypher, though we speak, we listen more than speak. We listen to what pours out of the hearts of others and become a part of the cypher's collective story.

So, let us keep on flowing, let us keep on manifesting hope in the world; for rest assured, a better day is on its way!

Check one! Check two!

NOTES

CHECK ONE, CHECK TWO

1. Mahatma Gandhi, 1869–1948
2. 49Tales, Comments, on the blog "George Zimmerman and God-Sponsored Racism," by Michael W. Waters, Huffington Post, July 23, 2012.

PART THREE: JUSTICE

1. Francis Bellamy, pledge to the American flag, 1892.

PART FOUR: POP CULTURE

1. Robin Sylvan, "Rap Music, Hip-Hop Culture, and 'The Future Religion of the World,'" in *God in the Details: American Religion in Popular Culture,* ed. Eric Michael Mazur and Kate McCarthy (New York: Routledge, 2001), 281–98.

KEEP FLOWING!

1. Donald K. McKim, *Westminster Dictionary of Theological Terms* (Louisville, KY: Westminster John Knox Press, 1996).

ABOUT THE AUTHOR

MICHAEL W. WATERS is founding pastor of Joy Tabernacle African Methodist Episcopal Church in Dallas, Texas, one of the newest and fastest-growing A.M.E. Churches in the state. As pastor, preacher, professor, author, motivational speaker, and community organizer, his words of hope and empowerment have inspired national and international audiences.

Featured in *EBONY* magazine as an emerging leader, Waters has shared his keen insights on such esteemed platforms as *The NBC Nightly News*, the British Broadcasting Corporation's *Newshour*, and National Public Radio. He holds a Bachelor of Arts degree, a Master of Divinity degree, and a Doctor of Ministry degree from Southern Methodist University. Waters is currently a Ph.D. student in Leadership Studies at Dallas Baptist University.

A sought-after preacher and lecturer, Waters has made numerous presentations before church, civic, collegiate, and corporate bodies on topics of interest ranging from Fortune 500 diversity practices and ethical leadership principles to the intersections of religion and hip-hop culture. His writings have appeared in such respected publications as the Huffington Post, *The African American Pulpit*, *Feasting on the Gospels*, and *Becoming Fire: Spiritual Writings from Rising Generations*.

Waters is married to Yulise Reaves Waters. They are the parents of three children: Michael Jeremiah, Hope Yulise, and Liberty Grace.

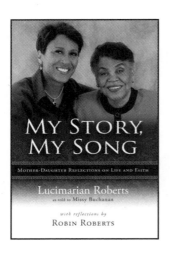

My Story, My Song

This heartwarming memoir of 88-year-old Lucimarian Roberts, mother of *Good Morning America*'s coanchor Robin Roberts, gives you a glimpse into pivotal moments in Mrs. Roberts' life, showing how faith in God has strengthened her and how God has guided and encouraged her through people of all ages and races.

My Story, My Song brings together the pivotal moments of Lucimarian Roberts' intriguing life with personal reflections from her daughter Robin.
#978-0-8358-1107-1

Reluctant Pilgrim

This is the spiritual memoir of a God-hungry woman trying to navigate her mixed desires, convictions, and disappointments. Enuma Okoro is a tea-sipping, seminary-educated young woman with a passion for God, close girlfriends, gorgeous shoes, and desire for a godly man with great hair. A fascinating story of longing, loss, and promise—and of God's presence through it all.
#978-1-935205-10-4

<u>TO ORDER</u>

Call: 1.800.972.0433 or go to Bookstore.UpperRoom.org